THE SECRETS OF SUCCESSFUL SALES MANAGEMENT

For a full list of Management Books 2000 titles visit our web-site on http://www.mb2000.com

THE SECRETS OF SUCCESSFUL SALES MANAGEMENT

Tony Adams

2000

Copyright © Anthony Adams 1987, 1999

First published in Great Britain in 1987 by William Heinemann Ltd

This new edition published 1999 by Management Books 2000 Ltd,
Cowcombe House,
Cowcombe Hill,
Chalford,
Gloucestershire GL6 8HP
Tel: 01285-760722. Fax: 01285-760708
e-mail: 106002.3004@compuserve.com

Printed and bound in Great Britain by Biddles, Guildford

British Library Cataloguing in Publication Data is available

ISBN 1-85252-283-6

Author's note
For grammatical reasons, in many parts of this book, the word 'salesman' has been used to mean salesman or saleswoman. The use of this word does not imply that saleswomen are not as effective as salesmen. In the author's experience, saleswomen are equally as effective and successful as salesmen.

Contents

Prologue

Regardless of their social or financial backgrounds there are some times when all men are equal. One is at birth, another is at death, and a third is when they are standing side by side in the gents' loo. It was on one such occasion (when I was neither being born nor dying) that I said to my boss, who was standing beside me, 'Why do you think we are so successful?'

He did not reply at once. It was not that he was so preoccupied that he did not hear me, it was simply because it was one of those thundery, hot and humid summer days when reactions slow down to the speed of international diplomacy. At last, he zipped up his fly, looked at me and said, 'It's because we are prepared to do what other people are not prepared to do'.

He washed his hands and left.

There are only a few such moments in a lifetime when an experience becomes a turning point, a benchmark, a watershed. And this for me was a watershed in more ways than one. I did not realize it at the time. In fact I wondered, what did he actually mean?

'We are prepared to do what other people are not prepared to do?'

I had been executive sales manager of Gross Cash Registers for some five years by then and, as it was my responsibility to manage the sales function, I suppose he was paying me a compliment by agreeing that we were more successful than others. The methods I used to achieve success did not fall upon me like manna from heaven. They had been begged, borrowed and stolen from others over the years or learned from my own bitter experience. I still continue to learn as the years go by and I never forget the basic requirement for success in sales management. You must be prepared to do what other people are not prepared to do.

1

Know Yourself

If you have read my first book, *The Secrets of Successful Selling*, you will know that I had no intention of being a sales manager when I left school. My first job was as a farmer's pupil. I lived in the farmhouse with the farmer, his wife and family and, although at that time I was the lowest form of animal life on the farm, I knew that for me this was a stepping stone on the road to farm management. This did not mean that I worked less hard than the farm workers, far from it. I was the first one up in the morning and the last one to get home at night.

It seems difficult to believe now but although the farm was only six miles from Aylesbury and five miles from Leighton Buzzard we had no mains water, no electricity, no mains gas and no mains drainage. We had to pump well water up into a tank in the roof every day for our domestic water supply. Pumping water for the livestock was an even more daunting daily task. The pump was not a mechanical device but a traditional hand pump which could be described as ye olde village pump. It required 700 strokes per day for the house and several thousand strokes per day for the stock, dependent on the season. I cannot remember the exact number, but I do remember that after the first thousand you broke through the pain barrier and started hallucinating.

Lighting was a combination of oil lamps and candles in the house, and hurricane lamps in the farm buildings. Bottled gas was used for cooking. The total absence of main drainage and the effort needed to pump water up to the tank in the roof meant that using the lavatory in the bathroom upstairs was discouraged. It was accepted that the women and children should take precedence, so the men of the family comprising The Governor (age 70), Master Will (age 36), and I (age 16) should make other arrangements. Normally, as bedtime approached, we would decide it was time to 'water the ferret' and we would visit the stables.

In the garden where one would normally expect to find a summer house there was a Victorian family loo affectionately known as the thunder box. The wooden seat of scrubbed and bleached pine was about six feet wide. In it were three oval holes. The dimensions of each were no doubt the result of considerable medical research designed to provide the perfect temporary resting place for Mother Bare, Father Bare, and Baby Bare.

I would love to tell you that it was well patronized, but in five years I never saw a single person use it, never mind a married couple and child.

Each morning at 6 o'clock I lit my candle, splashed a few drops of cold water from a bowl on my face, dressed and went downstairs. My first job was to make a pot of tea and give my boss and his wife a cup of tea in bed. I then sat in the kitchen alone warming my hands on the side of my pint mug as I sipped my hot tea. When the tea was finished it was time to check the stock. If you are a shopkeeper this means you check the goods on the shelves. If you are a farmer it means that you check to see that all the sheep, pigs, cattle, and horses are where they ought to be and are fit and well. For me this meant walking three miles round the farm counting the stock in every field and getting close enough to every one to see that it was in good health. If there were some sheep or cattle missing I had to find them and bring them back to the field they had left and then mend the gap in the fence through which they had escaped. You will realize that this was a job that had to be done every day of the year. Sometimes it was a joy on a summer's day with the lambs, the calves, and the inquisitive foals coming to me, curiosity overcoming their fear, nibbling and sucking the fingers of my outstretched hand. Sometimes it was hard work in the late autumn and winter months, humping bales of hay and oat straw to give them each an early morning feed. Sometimes it was pouring with rain.

In early spring there was lambing and there were not many days on which I did not find a ewe in trouble. To be able to cope with these problems and save the life of the ewe and lamb was immensely rewarding so I do not want you to think that it was all hard work for no reward. On the contrary, the job satisfaction was tremendous.

The townsman, driving along the motorway, sees sheep and cattle in the fields, and like the Chinese to Englishmen or Englishmen to the Chinese, the sheep and cattle all look alike to him, but to the farmer, every ewe, every lamb, and every heifer is different. I think the townsman knows that this is so but he probably does not realize how much this develops the farmer's sense of observation. He cannot only look at forty apparently identical ewes and recognize each one as an individual, although they have no names, but he can tell if they are well, not very well, sick, shortly to lamb, suffering from maggots, foot rot or too much clover. Although his sheep are nameless he can identify them. The wall-eyed ewe, the floppy-eared ewe, the descriptions are endless.

You would think the fields would be more difficult to identify. Not a bit of it. Every field has a name. Some names are descriptive and others have been handed down from generation to generation so that their meaning is lost in the mists of time. As I walked around the farm each morning checking the stock, I walked from Dairy Ground to the Front Meadow, into Long Meadow, and over the stile into Harris's Ground. I then checked the stock in Stephen's Meadow and over the brook on to Wing Hill and back into the Slad. Next stop was the Ten Acre Spinney and over the fence into Great Ground.

Not only was it possible to identify and know the history of each animal on the farm, not only was it possible to identify each field by name, but it was possible to identify every type of grass in every field. Lack of rye grass, needed for bulk of hay crop, meant nitrogen was needed. Lack of clover meant potash was needed. Other characteristics indicated excess of acidity, poor drainage. I learnt the value of close observation, the recognition of symptoms of the disease at an early stage, when a cure can still be effective.

I was normally back at the farmhouse for breakfast between 8 o'clock and 9 o'clock. That was before I started the normal day's work of ploughing, cultivating, sowing, harvesting, threshing, fencing, muck spreading, shearing, dipping, dependent upon the season. The day was punctuated by lunch and tea taken in the fields. Lunch was normally boiled bacon sandwiches and a quart of milk which I took with me on the tractor. Tea was usually brought into the field by pony and trap. I worked harder and longer than anyone else because I knew that if I were ever to be a successful farm manager I would have to earn the respect of the farm workers who would be working for me. To do that I would have to plough a straighter furrow, layer a better hedge, build a better rick, and these things I did. I also worked longer hours, until dark and beyond. I worked seven days a week.

Although I could not possibly have been aware of it at the time I was even then in possession of some of the essential secrets of successful sales management. How many of them have you identified?

- First, and most important, I knew within me that I was a manager, a leader.

- Second, I knew I had to be a better craftsman than the farm workers were themselves.

- Third, I had to work very long hours.

- Fourth, I enjoyed my work, I needed the job satisfaction.

- Fifth, I did not mind rolling up my sleeves and getting my hands dirty.

- Sixth, I was working for the future – I was aiming for greater responsibility, greater achievement.

- Seventh, I was caring for others – the stock and the land – genuinely caring, without altruistic motives, and yet I knew that above all I was involved in a business. If you care for the lambs, bring them safely into the world, ensure their mothers do not desert them, keep them free from foot rot, maggots, ticks, and liver fluke they fetch a higher price at auction for breeding stock or slaughter for the Sunday dinner market.

- Eighth, I was observant, recognizing problems before they became insoluble.

2

A proven method

Would you get up at 6 a.m. every morning, regardless of the weather, and work until 10 p.m. every night without shelter, for full board and four packets of cigarettes a week, if the future rewards and job satisfaction are there?

Are you prepared to do what other People are not prepared to do?

I was fortunate during my teenage years, because not only was I doing what I wanted to do, I was given the opportunity to meet a tremendously wide spectrum of people.

Obviously I worked very closely with the farm workers and identified with them. They had very little capital behind them, neither had I. They earned a subsistence wage, so did I. They had a love of the land, so had I. On these levels we could communicate.

There was, however, another level on which I found identification with my boss, the farmer. I was constantly looking for better, more cost effective ways of running the farm, even if it meant that we could operate with fewer employees.

The third level on which I found identification was that of leadership. Do not ask me how or why some people find it necessary to adopt the role of leader, I only know that if you gather together twelve good men and true there will be a foreman. If you form a political party there will be several people vying for the leadership. You will know instinctively if you are a leader. The fact that you bought this book is a good indication that you are a leader. When you bought it you probably thought I was going to tell you about the many management techniques that could be classified as 'the secrets of successful sales management'. You were right. I am going to explain in detail many of the sales management techniques which could legitimately be described as the secrets of successful sales management. The advice must fall on fertile ground, and therefore the first secret of successful sales management is that you must be an instinctive manager, a natural leader, someone who can earn respect, someone who can command loyalty, and if you cannot get people to work that way then you must be prepared to use the KITA (kick-in-the-arse) technique.

Unfortunately promotion into management seldom comes to those who are best qualified. No matter what the craft, no matter what the profession, promotion into management goes to the best craftsman, the best professional, not necessarily to the best potential manager. The best salesman is offered promotion into sales management because he is the best salesman. It happened to me.

The leap for me from farm management to salesmanship was a quantum leap, it was the biggest leap possible, 12,000 miles from England to Australia. A new career, a new life.

I explained how it happened in *The Secrets of Successful Selling*, but if you have not read that book it will help you to understand that transition if I explain that I was managing a farm in Northamptonshire for a widow who decided to sell up and join her children who had migrated to Australia.

As I had nothing better to do I followed her example. I had no ties and no responsibilities, so I bought a ticket and sailed half way round the world into a new life. It is not easy to re-establish yourself in a new country with no friends, no relatives, and no relevant qualifications, for a British farm manager is as irrelevant in Australia as a madam in a convent.

Thanks to some generous young Australians I met on the ship, I was offered a job as a taxi driver. The only problem was that I did not have a taxi driver's licence. You may know that London taxi drivers have to acquire *the Knowledge* before they can be granted a licence. The Knowledge is a knowledge of London. A detailed knowledge that ensures that a passenger, stating his destination, would be taken by the shortest possible route. Aspiring London taxi drivers spend many weeks on a motor scooter with a clipboard mounted on the handlebars, learning the knowledge, so that they can pass the test and be awarded the coveted licence.

A similar system pertains in Melbourne, Australia, so when I was invited to apply for a job as a taxi driver the first thing I had to do was to obtain *the Knowledge*.

I did not buy a motor scooter and a clipboard, I bought a street map of Melbourne. I burned the midnight oil. In fact I read that map all night. I thought of nothing else. I repeated to myself again and again the names of the streets I would use to travel from Spencer Street Station to Heidelberg, from Spring Street to Toorak, from St Kilda to Moonee Pond.

I finally got to sleep at about 4 a.m.

At 10 o'clock the next morning I reported to the Exhibition Buildings where the test was to be held. The examiner asked the right questions and I passed. It is ridiculous but true. I had never seen any of the places to which I was now licensed to transport paying passengers, but although I had no idea what they looked like I knew how to get there. I worked on night shift for three years, made money, bought a car, got married, bought a house, sold my cab and became a salesman.

Within six months I was the best encyclopaedia salesman in the Melbourne branch of George Newnes (Aust.) Pty Limited, and they needed a manager.

Did they advertise for a successful manager? No. They offered me the job because I was the best salesman.

I accepted the job because the offer was a compliment. My ego was inflated and most of all because I knew that I had to. It was an essential part of my psyche. Can you imagine me saying 'I don't think I should accept because I am not qualified to be a manager, I am a salesman'. Some people may react that way but not me. Even if you can imagine that happening I can assure you it did not. I went home that night ten feet tall and told my wife I had been promoted. She was delighted and so was I.

This scene is being enacted every day in countless homes throughout the country, and sadly in many cases it will be the first step on the road to disappointment and disillusion. But fortunately for those who understand what management is all about, and for those that are eager to learn, it will be the first step on the road to successful sales management and tremendous job satisfaction.

If you take any technician, a bio-chemist, a surveyor, an engineer, his experience as a technician or specialist does little to equip him as a manager. His only route for promotion is through the ranks of management. This is one of the reasons put forward for the British malaise. It is a widely held belief that people are promoted progressively into more demanding roles until they reach a level at which they are incompetent, and there they stay.

Many of the personality traits that a manager needs are those you will find in a successful salesman, so the success rate in promoting salesmen into management should be greater than in many other crafts and professions. It is tragic however that many salesmen promoted into management are not aware of this basic fact. If you were to say to newly appointed sales managers 'Treat your employees as if they were potential customers', and they took your advice, they would probably be successful. Unfortunately most books on sales management and most company disciplines and directives advise or instruct sales management to treat their staff as if they were 'other ranks' in the army, to be disciplined, drilled, and punished if they step out of line. Potentially successful salesmen are people who can control and influence the potential customers to whom they sell. They have tremendous self confidence, they regard their territories as fields in which they sow the seeds and harvest the crop.

They must be disciplined certainly, because creative people are often weak on organization, but they must be supported, instructed, and above all respected.

In *The Secrets of Successful Selling* I made it abundantly clear that to be successful a salesman needs talent and this must be respected, but in addition he needs training and management. I shall illustrate how a similar combination of qualities and disciplines are necessary for successful sales management. Talent is within the manager, as I knew when I was a farmer's pupil. My mind was preoccupied with more cost effective ways of running the farm. I identified as a manager. This was not a pose. This was not an attitude I had been instructed to adopt. It was me.

If you have accepted promotion into management for the increased status, the increased salary, or because you could not really refuse, then I suggest you use this book as a firelighter because you are not a natural manager. Such advice as is within its pages would fall on stony ground.

If you accepted promotion because you knew it was the logical progression into management, your true vocation, then you will find the following chapters will confirm your own views or teach you something new or provoke you into examining your reasons for disagreeing with me.

I have never regarded information on sales management as suitable material for a bonfire. On the contrary, I have read books, I have been to countless seminars and conferences from which I have learnt a great deal. It is also interesting to note that many of the lessons I learnt were learnt by the mistakes of other people to whom I had to report.

Whenever I was demotivated by a word, a memo, a letter, or a discipline, I learnt something. I learnt that if I were to be a successful manager I would have to find a way of achieving the desired end result without demotivation. I knew one simple fact when I accepted my first promotion into sales management and that was that my future progress, my future prosperity, would depend on my ability to increase the business generated by my sales team within the financial constraints imposed by the company.

I had not at that time been subjected to any demotivating

influences so my approach was very simplistic and positive. There were as I saw it three ways in which I could increase business.

1. I could enlarge the sales force.
2. I could increase the number of calls made by the existing members of the team.
3. I could increase the quality of each sales presentation.

What is more, I was sufficiently big-headed to believe that I could do all these things. I was not sufficiently experienced at that time to recognize one of *the* most important secrets of successful sales management, which is that you must have a detailed, proven method of selling your product or service which, if performed meticulously by *average* sales people, will result in sales at an acceptable sales cost.

When I talk about methods of selling I am talking about the whole sales process, from identifying the market, contacting the decision maker to obtaining the sales interview, and obtaining and documenting the order.

Many companies fail because they employ 'salesmen' to sell an excellent product or service without having a detailed, well proven method of selling that product or service which can be taught to the salesmen they engage.

I have always regarded salesmen as being closely related to actors and they are. Many of them move from company to company and are employed to generate revenue for their employers by getting the public to 'buy tickets'. Can you imagine what would happen if you employed four actors and said 'I want you to act in a play which is about twin brothers marrying twin sisters. One couple are very much in love whilst the other couple hate each other's guts. The unhappy wife decides to poison her husband but poisons her brother-in-law by mistake. To cover up her mistake she has to persuade the husband she hates to pretend to be her brother-in-law and take up residence with her sister thereby getting rid of him that way. How she does this is the climax of the third act'.

They would probably say 'It's a great plot but where is the script and which theatre are we playing?'

A successful sales manager has to recruit salesmen and say:
'This is the plot.'
'This is the script.'
'This is where you perform.'

In addition the successful sales manager, unlike the theatrical entrepreneur, has to be prepared to teach the new recruit how to act, and this is an art in itself.

3

Observation – attention to detail

I have now identified two of the secrets of successful sales management. The first is that the successful sales manager must know that he is a manager and must *know* he is a leader. The second is that he must have a proven, successful method of selling the product or service that can be taught to the average salesman who will perform, subject to good management, at a level that is within the company's financial constraints.

When I joined George Newnes I had been a successful farm manager and a successful hire car proprietor, but I had had no sales training. I had been trained as a commercial radio announcer, an experience which has been invaluable to me ever since, but none of this experience would have enabled me to sell encyclopaedias from door to door from day 1. I did sell encyclopaedias from day 1 because when I joined George Newnes I was told:

1. Who to contact.
2. How to contact them.
3. What to say to get an appointment.
4. How to present the benefits.
5. How to close the sale.
6. How to document the sale.

If you are to be a successful salesman you must know the answers to these six questions. If you are to be a successful sales manager you must define the answers to the six questions and be capable of training sales staff in each of these areas of responsibility. If you are already a sales manager it would be a good idea for you to check against that checklist and see if you are already defining the answers to these questions. Each one is a major sales management responsibility.

I was fortunate in that I was eased into these complex areas by a well organized professional company. Obviously the simplistic methods they used did not equip me with the sales management – skills I required in more complex companies that I joined subsequently, but let us look at these vital questions:

1 Who to contact

George Newnes were selling encyclopaedias. Their market was the family with children of school age. How do you locate families with children of school age?

Well no doubt there are sophisticated methods based on computer predictions, the electoral register, and other hi-tech techniques. George Newnes were not into hi-tech. They employed old-age pensioners to call on all households and ask 'Do you have any children of school age? What are their names and ages?' Having obtained this information they were often asked 'Why do you want to know', to which they would reply 'It is just a survey of children in the area'.

This simple procedure produced lists of potential customers at a cost of 21 pence per name. Not only were the prospects 'qualified' (they were not just names, they were names of families with children of school age together with the children's forenames and ages). What is more they were listed geographically.

2 How to contact them

It is essential to devise a method of working that reduces the amount of travelling time to a minimum. It is very common for salesmen to spend no more than two hours per day in a face-to-face selling situation. This does not mean that they are in the betting shop, or on the golf course, or in some lady's bedroom, but because their management has not devised a more effective way of working. I have not found a way of getting salesmen to be in a selling situation for more than four hours per day, but this is a 100 per cent increase on what is the norm in many companies. At George Newnes our selling hours were limited to the hours when both mother and father were at home and willing to see us. Usually that was between 6 p.m. and 10 p.m. on weekdays plus weekends and public holidays, so we had to make the most of those valuable hours. It concentrates the mind when the time is limited.

At that time, in the state of Victoria, pub licensing hours were very limited. In fact, pubs (or hotels as they are known in Australia) had to close their bars at 6 p. m. Most workers finished work at 5.30 p.m. so their minds were concentrated on drinking as much as possible between 5.30 and 6 p. m.

The traditional story tells of eight factory workers racing through the factory gates, across the road and into the hotel. The first person through the swing doors arrives at the bar and shouts 'Eight beers please mate'. He then turns to the next man to arrive and asks 'And what are you drinking, sport?' You may think this is an exaggeration but it is not. They knew they only had one chance of being served between 5.30 and 6 p. m., so on that one occasion they had to order enough beer to top up their blood alcohol level for the next twenty-four hours, and what was more difficult, to drink it in thirty minutes or less.

The result was predictable. At 6 p.m. they were ejected from the cool shade of the bar into the Australian sunlight. Some made the journey to the tram, the bus, or the train which carried them home to disgusted, long-suffering wives and children. The rest fell down on the grass verges by the side of the road outside the hotel and slept it off. Mercifully, an enlightened State Parliament has changed the licensing laws in Victoria, so the '6 o'clock swill' as it was known is now a thing of the past, but the lesson it taught us all is still with us.

If a commodity is in short supply it is more highly valued than if it is plentiful. The commodity we are talking about in this context is selling time. If your only chance of selling is between 6.00 and 10 p.m. you make the most of those hours, as I did with George Newnes. But similarly if the commodity is territory then the smaller the territory the more the salesman will value the territory he has.

This concept is examined in more detail in later chapters. It was in these very early days in my sales management career that I learnt this secret of successful sales management. Limit your salesman's opportunities either by territory size, by hours of work, by type of prospect, or by type of product, so that he values each prospect more highly than he otherwise would and therefore puts substantially more effort into each sales opportunity.

Because our opportunities were limited by time we packed in as many appointments as we could between those hours. To do this we had to go out calling at about 4 p.m., explaining to the mothers that we wanted to call on them when their husbands were home to discuss with them a new educational aid for the children. Our aim was to arrange appointments for 10, 9.30, 9, 8.30, 8, 7.30, 7, 6.30, and 6 p.m. To do this we had to start work at 4 p. m. and often did not complete our last presentation until 11 p.m. We were therefore working for seven hours plus travelling time per day but our minds were concentrated on the vital selling hours of 6 to 10 p.m.

Had we not been so well directed we would have spent some of those valuable hours travelling, but as it was we often stayed in one street all night.

Naturally this list of names and addresses not only enabled us to use time to the best advantage, it enabled us to personalize the call. When the doorbell was answered we could say 'Good evening, Mrs Farnes-Barnes, my name is Adams. I have been asked to call on you sometime when Mr Farnes-Barnes is home, to discuss with you both a new educational plan for Marlon and Marilyn. Will you both be home if I call back at about 9.30?'

So when I took over as sales manager of the Melbourne branch much of my job had been done for me.

1. I knew who to contact.
2. I knew how to contact them.
3. I knew what to say to get an appointment.

In fact the rest had been done for me too.

Every new salesman joining the company was given a slim booklet which was 'the script'. It gave the salesman the exact words to use from start to finish and what is more, there were none of those smart alec phrases that some sales trainers teach new salesmen to use.

I was recently visited by two salesmen from different companies selling different products in response to two enquiries that I had made. Each one of them began their sales presentation by saying 'Before I begin, can I have your agreement that you will make a firm decision, yes or no, before I leave you this evening.' In each case I said 'No you can't.'

When they asked me 'Why not', I told them I had asked another company for information and I would not make a decision until I had evaluated both proposals. One salesman left without opening his briefcase, the other said 'Oh all right then, I'll press on but I know what the answer will be'.

He was right, the answer was 'No', because the proposition put to me was financially unsound – a con. That was why he needed 'sales techniques'.

George Newnes were more professional. They knew that the main reason people buy from a particular person or from a particular company is because they have confidence in that person or company. They also knew that if people buy a product or service it is to fill a need.

That need can be very obvious. For example, people buy a drink because they are thirsty, or food because they are hungry. They also buy to fill a need that can be less obvious. They buy an expensive painting because they think it will give them prestige, will earn them respect and admiration from others, but you would find it difficult to sell them a valuable painting on those grounds.

You would probably do better by selling them the need to invest wisely and enjoy capital gains rather than investment income.

Whatever the product or service you are selling you have to lay a foundation on which the benefits can be built, and George Newnes knew that the foundation on which the desire for an encyclopaedia could be built was the parents' natural desire to give their children a good education.

The script, however, covered every eventuality – even getting in the door. I do not care what product or service you are selling, you have difficulty getting face to face with the *MAN*. He is the person who has *m*eans, the *a*uthority, and the *n*eed.

When I was selling encyclopaedias the problem was not making the appointment with Mrs Farnes-Barnes because all you had to ask was 'Will you both be home about 9.30?' (not 'Would you like me to call'?). The problem was Mr Farnes-Barnes. When you called back at 9.30 he would come to the door and say 'Well, what's it all about then?'

The script said 'Well, it's something to show you, can I come in for a minute?'

He would say 'Well show me now.'

The script said 'The only reason I am here now is so that I can see you and Mrs Farnes-Barnes together. It won't take long, can I come in for a minute?'

The golden rule was 'Don't open your briefcase on the doorstep'.

This was the final part of stage three, how to overcome the objections to getting an appointment.

3 How to present the benefits

The only way I can tell you how I was taught to lay the foundations for benefits is to quote from *The Secrets of Successful Selling* page 25.

'I am sure you feel, as I do, that education is vitally important these days, don't you Mrs Jones?' Pause for agreement.

'And you probably know that classes in school are so large that teachers can spend very little time with each pupil to give them individual attention, Yes?'

Pause to get the parents to respond and then personalize the demonstration.

'How many children are there in John's class, Mrs Jones?'

'We think there are 42.'

'42! And what about Mary?'

'About the same, I think.'

'My word! That's why you at home can play such an important part in your children's education. But teaching methods have changed so much since we were at school, haven't they? They don't even teach them the alphabet do they? It's all ker and der.'

'Obviously you want to help your children but it's difficult unless you know how. True? Well that's where *Pictorial Knowledge* comes in.'

Yes, I was exceptionally fortunate when I was first appointed to the bottom rung of the management stepladder. I was given the distillate, the spirit of professional salesmanship, not in a glass but on a plate. How many salesmen are told that before you sell a benefit you must establish a need? Stated as simply as that it is obvious, but most salesmen are so preoccupied extolling the virtues of their products they forget that the person they are selling to does not realize he has a need.

When I was running sales training courses for Gross Cash Registers I used to tell the salesmen on the course that I knew a small business, a manufacturer not far from the office, that sold ladies' underwear at very reasonable prices, if you called at the factory. I asked if any of the salesmen (they were all men in those days) were into ladies' underwear. None of them admitted that they were.

I then asked how many of them were married. All the worried looking ones raised their hands. I then asked them if they thought it would be a nice idea to take a present home to their wives at the end of the week, as a peace offering.

All of them except the Geordies and the Scots thought it would be a good idea (I am only joking). I then asked if they would like to buy something straight from the factory at trade prices. They all agreed they would, including the Geordies and the Scots (I am still joking), and so I had laid the foundation for a sale.

I had not really. There was no manufacturer of unmentionables anywhere near our offices as far as I knew, but I had illustrated the point. You must lay the foundation for the need before you can sell the benefit that fills that need. I had learned that basic fact from George Newnes.

I was also taught how necessary it is to get your prospect to agree that there is not only a need but that the benefit fills that need. We will discuss this most important aspect of selling benefits later.

4 How to close the sale

Finally, I was given a simple, no-holds-barred, method for closing the sale. It was not 'Do you want to buy?' It was not 'Do you prefer the red or the green?' It was:

'I am sure you know that encyclopaedias are very expensive. Our own Chambers encyclopaedia can cost £400.00. *Pictorial Knowledge* is nothing like that. It is not even £100.00.'

'It is only £32.00, but even that can be spread out over 32 months for no extra charge.'

'Some people pay as much as £5.00 deposit and £3.00 a month, but you can pay as little as £1.00 deposit and £1.00 a month.'

'Most people start off with £3.00. How does £3.00 sound to you Mrs Jones, about right?'
On confirmation that £3.00 was 'about right' the pen started writing and entered the deposit. The sale was closed.

5 How to document the sale

Although it was the salesman's job to enter the deposit and the monthly payments, the rest of the order form had to be completed by the customer. He had to fill this out in his *own handwriting*. He had to give his name, address, occupation, employer, the time in present employment, and his age in *words*. He was also required to initial a clause in heavy type which said *This is a firm order and not subject to cancellation by me.*

As a young sales manager I was not required to initiate these procedures. I had only to implement them. As a salesman, I privately questioned the company's insistence on the customer completing the order form in his own handwriting. Surely the salesman could do this just as efficiently? We were not allowed to sell to people under 21 years of age and I did not realize how easy it would be for a salesman to change the number 19 to number 49 if the age had been entered as numerals and not words, but once I had been promoted to branch manager it was only a matter of months before I had lost my innocence. I learned why the company wanted the customer to complete the order form in his own handwriting.

One of my best salesmen whom I shall call Adam, had a matrimonial problem. His problem was 5 feet 2 inches tall; 8 stone 7 pounds, blonde, 35-24-35, whom I shall call Eve.

He moved out of the matrimonial home in Melbourne, deserting his wife and children, and took up residence in a caravan with his paramour near the far South Eastern Victorian town of Eden close to Lake's Entrance and the Ninety Mile Beach.

He continued to sell *Pictorial Knowledge* at his normal rate of seven sales per week. I have already told you that the standard closing technique that was used was to get the prospect to decide on the size of the deposit. Some paid £1.00, some paid £5.00, but most paid £3.00. The salesman's commission ranged from £5.00 to £7.00 dependent on performance, so in theory, in the short term, the salesman could make a profit by forging an order, paying a £1.00 deposit and thereby being paid £7.00 commission. Obviously, in time, he would be found out, but when needs must the devil drives.

Adam was forging these orders and paying the deposits himself and I did not realize it. I was still innocent, I trusted everyone. He was clever. He used different pens, he wrote in different styles, and no doubt his partner lent a hand as well inventing names and addresses and possibly completing some of the order forms.

I paid him his commission as the orders arrived and the company despatched books to the railhead which was still some seventy miles short of Eden. The station master there stacked the boxes – seven boxes per week – in the parcels office where they remained awaiting collection.

It is difficult to know how long this would have gone on had not the company launched a special promotion *Newnes Pictorial Knowledge* plus *The New Imperial Dictionary* – a combined order at a concessionary price.

The commission was £1.25 more on the combined order than on *Pictorial Knowledge* alone. This proved irresistible to Adam who was unable to support Eve in Eden and his wife in Melbourne. The combined orders came flooding in and the company despatched *Pictorial Knowledge* and *The New Imperial Dictionary* to every new customer. For convenience of packaging and to enjoy the most favourable delivery rates *Pictorial Knowledge* was still despatched by rail but the dictionary was posted by recorded delivery.

Within a matter of days head office was having dictionaries returned by the post office with the advice that there was no such address or if the address did exist that the addressee did not exist and the occupant of the premises was not prepared to accept delivery.

This action by the post office prompted head office to tell me that they held me responsible if these orders were not genuine, therefore it was up to me to recover either the property or alternatively the full retail price.

This did not give me a great deal of choice when you consider that there were dozens of sets of encyclopaedias stacked in a Victoria railway parcels office in the middle of nowhere at a value of £32.00 per parcel.

I hesitated for seven or eight minutes then bought a ticket for the end of the line!

If you are a European you will have heard of the butter mountain and the beef mountain. When I stepped off that train at the end of the line my view of the most beautiful stretch of Victoria coastline was obscured by an encyclopaedia mountain. The dictionaries which had been the catalyst were all gone and it was not long before I had consigned the encyclopaedia mountain back to Sydney.

Although I had thereby achieved the purpose of my errand I felt compelled to continue on to the caravan site from which Adam and Eve were operating. The only means of transport was a taxi, and within two hours I was talking to a pretty 5 foot 2 inch blonde at the door of a caravan, with two children whose ages I would guess at two and three, clutching at her skirt with sticky fingers.

Adam had gone. She had no idea where he was.

What could I do?

The taxi was waiting – I returned to the railhead.

I never saw Adam again and I sometimes wonder what happened to him. I am grateful to him in one way because he taught me a valuable lesson. He taught me that not only are we all, like Adam, subject to temptation but a percentage of us will succumb to it.

It is very easy for managers to look down on the 'other ranks' and say 'Well, what else can you expect', but it was no time at all before one of my peers, another branch manager in Victoria, gave in to temptation.

It was a normal summer's day. The temperature was in the 80s and we had no air conditioning. To make matters worse everyone wore a worsted suit and a collar and tie, so that meant that I had to as well. I sat behind my desk taking the regular telephone calls generated by recruitment advertising.

Suddenly, one call was different. It was from my boss, Ray Eaton, calling from Sydney.

'Mr Adams,' he said.

'Yes,' I replied.

'I want you to listen carefully.'

I remained silent but the hairs on the back of my neck marched upward like a millipede's legs. I shivered.

'I want you to go into Mr Haywood's office and say 'Mr Eaton has just telephoned me and has told me to ask you for your keys to the safe'.

'Do you understand?'

'Yes', I said.

'I am getting the next plane to Melbourne so I should be with you by about 2 p.m. Don't open the safe, just hold the keys until I get to you, Okay?'

'Okay,' I said. I put my telephone back on its rest and made two plus two equal five. Obviously Brian Haywood had been embezzling. What would he do when I asked him for the keys to the safe. Would he give them to me? Would he run? Would he hit me? Would he tell me to get stuffed?

I was not shivering any more, I was sweating. I knew I had to do what Ray Eaton had asked me to do, so I got up and went straight into Brian's office. He looked up as I entered, slightly surprised because I did not often visit him. He said 'Hello Tony, what can I do for you?'

The situation was, for me, totally unreal. I was sleepwalking but the words came out.

'Ray Eaton has just telephoned me and asked me to ask you for your keys to the safe'.

Slowly his eyes, which until then had been confident, aggressive, in contact with mine, lowered until he was staring at the blotter on his desk. The silence went on for ever. After about fifteen seconds he reached into his righthand trouser pocket, drew out the keys, and offered them to me without raising his head.

I went back to my office and stared at my blotter.

Ray Eaton arrived, as expected, at 2 p.m. He came straight into my office.

'Have you Mr Haywood's keys,' he asked.

'Yes,' I replied.

'Have you opened the safe today?'

'No,' I replied.

'Good, then let's get this over with, come on let's go.'

We went into Brian's office and Ray Eaton said 'I have here your cash return for the last week which says that you have seven hundred pounds cash in hand. As you know, Mr Adams has your safe keys, which you gave to him this morning. Mr Adams, will you please open the safe and give me Mr Haywood's cash box.'

I did as I was told.

'Thank you Mr Adams. Mr Haywood, can I have your key to this cash box please?'

'It's on the keyring I gave to Tony' he replied.

I gave Ray Eaton the keyring and he opened the cash box.

It was empty.

The story that Brian told was that he was unhappy about leaving his cash box in a safe when two other managers (I was one) had a key to the safe. He had therefore paid all his surplus cash into his girlfriend's bank account.

His girlfriend did in fact give the company seven hundred pounds described as replacement of George Newnes funds deposited for safe keeping. There was no reference to bookmakers .

Brian Haywood resigned.

There are so many lessons I learned from George Newnes that it is difficult to catalogue them.

I knew I was a manager before I joined them, but then they taught me that to be successful you must give your sales force the formula for success.

1. Who to contact.
2. How to contact them.
3. What to say to get an appointment.
4. How to present benefits.
5. How to close the sale.
6. How to document the sale.

Furthermore it must be a formula that can be taught to the average recruit.

I also learned that the habit of close observation which I had learned on the farm must be applied to sales management. I learned that lesson by default. I should have recognized Adam's sales as forgeries. I should have been looking at every member of my team every day to see that they were fit and well.

I did not resent the company holding me responsible for Adam's forgeries. I am grateful to them for not asking me to repay the commissions I paid him, although they naturally recovered the commission I had been paid on those spurious orders.

So now we have a third secret of successful sales management – close observation and attention to detail.

4

Recruitment – generating response

It could be argued that the most important responsibility of the sales manager is to recruit the right people. I would not disagree with that argument. But when you think about it, it is an admission that there are 'right people' and therefore 'wrong people'.

Obviously the 'right people' are not necessarily right for every type of sales appointment. In some cases, a professional qualification is absolutely essential. In others it is an in-depth knowledge of a specialized subject. In many cases, no previous experience is relevant.

In my experience technical knowledge is usually a liability rather than an asset for a salesman because he is then unable to resist the temptation to 'impress' the prospect by blinding him with science instead of selling the benefits. So how can we identify the right people?

The first lesson I learned was when I found myself looking for a job, in Melbourne, after I had sold my taxi. My qualifications and experience were easily defined. I was an out-of-work taxi-driver who could milk a cow.

As I read the 'Situations Vacant' columns in the Melbourne Age I read the headings to the advertisements, the words in bold type. Sometimes they were large display advertisements with headings like:

COMPANY SECRETARY

or:

HGV DRIVER

Sometimes they were classified ads with just one or two words in heavier type:

Secretary required by ....

or:

Book-keeper ....

I did not apply for any of those jobs because I knew I had no qualifications. I was not a company secretary, an HGV driver, a secretary, or a book-keeper. What would be the point in applying when there would be many other applicants who were qualified.

Even the advertisements headed:

SALESMAN

did not stimulate me to respond because I was not a salesman.

I am not implying that if you are recruiting salesmen you should not under any circumstances use an advertisement that is headed 'Salesman' because if you do, you will get applications from salesmen.

What I am saying is that people scanning the 'Situations Vacant' columns will not read the body copy of your advertisement unless they are able to identify with or are intrigued by the heading.

I responded to an advertisement that said:

Representative required by international publishing house. No previous experience required as full training will be given. Excellent opportunity for career advancement together with generous remuneration. Please telephone for an appointment.

What they really wanted were salesmen prepared to work every evening and all day Saturday and Sunday selling encyclopaedias door to door.

I responded to the advertisement because I did not know what a publisher's representative was. I thought he read books and, because it said 'no previous experience required' and as I had no previous experience, I applied.

George Newnes knew that there are far more 'right people' with no previous experience in sales on the labour market than there are 'right people' with experience. All the 'right people' with experience are carving careers for themselves with their present employers. Most salesmen looking for another salesman's job are drifters moving from job to job, always believing that the grass on the other side of the fence is greener.

Of course there are exceptions. There are some salesmen on the labour market for very good reasons, but they are looking for a *better* job, and what that means, only that salesman himself could tell you.

It might mean that he dislikes his boss or has no respect for him. It might mean that he thinks his employer is going bust. It might mean he has been spending most of his time away from home and wants to see his family more often. It might mean that he is being underpaid. It might mean he is looking for promotion but there are no opportunities where he is. It might mean that he has no faith in the product he is selling.

Whatever the reason he gives for wanting to change his job he is a bad bet unless he is in the top 50 per cent of his existing sales force. He must be *above average*, and I will come back to that later.

George Newnes knew that they could not attract above average salesmen. The hours were unsocial. The salary was non-existent, and security of employment depended upon last week's figures.

35

So they wrote their recruitment advertisements in such a way that the literate but naive reader would be attracted to them.

I have never forgotten the simple fact that I, with no previous sales experience and no conscious desire to be a salesman, started my successful, lifetime career in sales as a result of that simple advertisement that appeared in the *Melbourne Age* in 1953 and with which I identified.

I can only speak from my own experience which is predominantly in direct, speciality sales. By that I mean I have nearly always sold a product or service to a person who did not realize he needed the product or service I was selling until he met me, and having bought from me, never saw me again.

Put another way, you could say that I meet happy people and make them unhappy so that I can make them happy again.

There is absolutely no doubt in my mind that salesmen who can do this day after day, week after week, year after year and enjoy it, have a talent. They do not know that they have this talent until it is given the opportunity to manifest itself. It is impossible to know for sure if someone has this talent until they have been recruited and get out there, face to face with potential customers. But there are additional qualities successful salesmen nearly always possess, and conversely there are negative attributes which prevent otherwise potentially successful salesmen from succeeding, so the recruitment process can be partly scientific but partly pure intuition.

Apart from my three years with George Newnes when the advertisements were already defined by the management and you recruited anyone who would start, my first serious recruitment exercise was with Gross Cash Registers whom I joined in 1961. Whether I was successful or not can best be measured by the fact that when I joined them they had a sales force of 100 men and when I left them in 1969 it had risen to 500.

We had a turnover of almost 100 per cent, excluding management, so in simple terms we were recruiting between 80 and 400 men a year to keep the sales force up to strength.

This did not mean that we were replacing the whole sales force every year; far from it, we had a hard core of some 20 per cent that was successful, earning good money, liking the product, and happy to stay with the company for many years.

But the other 80 per cent, declining as the years went by, came and went, slightly faster than once a year on average. Even this 80 per cent were not all the same. Some could not sell, some would not work hard enough, some could sell but due to circumstances beyond their control could not continue working a full five-day week, and because of the huge numbers of people recruited, thousands over the year with Gross and with Ansafone, I was able to define the profile of the person we should *no*t recruit.

I looked at all the failures and by close examination and questioning I was able to establish, factually, some of the factors that contributed to a person's failure, and those findings appear later in this chapter. But what was even more important was that I was learning how to write an advertisement that would get the 'right people' to respond.

The wording of the advertisement was critical because although I did not require the applicant to have previous experience or academic qualifications, I needed him to be an energetic, enthusiastic, mentally alert, arrogant individual with a tremendous need for success in everything he undertook; the sort of person who believes that if a job is worth doing it is worth doing well.

If you apply those standards to the successful salesmen you know you will find that they have these qualities.

Obviously I did not want to turn away, or discourage, genuinely successful salesmen who were looking for a change of direction, and whereas at George Newnes the job was not sufficiently attractive to these people, at Gross Cash Registers and at Ansafone it was.

I therefore set about wording advertisements that would be read by experienced salesmen and also by people with no previous experience but with a desire to find a mentally stimulating and financially rewarding career.

I must confess that whenever I have written an advertisement that was addressed specifically to salesmen the quality of the applications was poor. Over 80 per cent of the salesmen reading the 'Situations Vacant' columns are other firms' failures, people we would not wish to recruit.

So I have used open advertisements that would allow anyone to apply, and by describing the type of applicant that we were looking for I have been able to eliminate some of the rubbish.

But first, we have to get them to read it and that depends on the heading:

In the first week of January:

A HAPPY NEW CAREER.

Looking for salesmen with a stable home life:

IS YOUR HUSBAND A SUCCESSFUL SALESMAN?

Looking for an age group:

IF YOU WERE BORN BETWEEN 1st APRIL 1949 AND 31st DECEMBER 1960, READ ON.

Just to get them reading it:

A RUT IS A SHALLOW GRAVE.

To appeal to both groups:

WHAT ABOUT A NEW CAREER IN SALES?

For the money hungry:

IF YOU THINK YOU ARE WORTH MORE THAN £20,000 p.a. YOU PROBABLY ARE.

As my objective was to build a large sales force and as my turnover of salesmen was high, I needed to generate as many applications as possible. There are not that many good, honest salesmen wanting to change their jobs today and there were not then either, but there were, without doubt, thousands of people out there with the natural talent a salesman needs and, all else being equal, I have found the inexperienced recruit every bit as successful after training as the experienced salesman.

To get a large response you need a large advertisement in a high circulation newspaper which has a reputation for recruitment advertisements, so that was the type of paper I normally used. But sometimes I had a need to recruit in one or two provincial areas only and on those occasions I used the local newspapers.

I remember one occasion when I advertised in an East Anglian newspaper, stating that I would be interviewing all the next day at the best hotel in town. 'Please phone Mr Adams on Norwich . . . (the hotel's telephone number) after 9 a. m.' The response to the advertisement was beyond my wildest dreams. Not only did the telephone in my bedroom start ringing shortly after 8 o'clock but the hotel switchboard and many of the selectors in the Norwich exchange were jammed until after 10 a.m.

It was a desperate experience for the hotel with all lines busy for two hours and no one able to telephone in or out. I was not popular, but there was nothing they could do about it. I did recruit the man I was looking for and he stayed with the company for many years, so fortunately I did not need to repeat the exercise. The hotel, for some reason, refused to allow their telephone number to appear in recruitment advertisements after that.

If you are recruiting specialists, it is comparatively easy to choose the media in which to place the advertisement. For example, if you need a financial director you will use the *Financial Times*, one of the heavy Sunday papers, and possibly one of the accountancy journals. If you are looking for a computer programmer you will advertise in some of the widely read computer papers.

But I could not say for sure what paper or even what part of what paper my potential salesmen would read because they came from all kinds of backgrounds and often did not really know what they were looking for when they stumbled across my advertisement. I therefore used a wide variety of media.

I used the national dailies, particularly the *Daily Telegraph* in

England, but also the Scottish and Welsh papers and a vast number of provincial evening papers like the *Liverpool Echo* and the *Leicester Mercury*.

I also discovered that some people identify with full display advertisements but others are somewhat daunted by them. They read the semi-display and the classified; other people with an entrepreneurial disposition will read the business opportunities columns; others will read the cards in the Job Centre windows.

I therefore wrote appropriate copy for each of these situations. The copy that went into the semi-display and classified ads was a précis of the display advertisement copy which usually read something like the following if I was trying to attract people with previous sales experience:

DO YOU RECKON YOU ARE A GOOD SALESMAN?

If you are looking for a company that recognizes the importance of the sales force and respects and rewards them accordingly then we fit the bill.

We pay a generous salary plus commission and bonus and provide a company car that can be used for unlimited family motoring. Pension, BUPA, and four weeks paid holiday are all part of the package. Opportunities for promotion into management are real after one year of service.

What do we ask in return?

Something we all share, 100 per cent loyalty, enthusiasm, and the determination needed to make our company the most successful company in our industry. If you would like to be one of us phone . . . to arrange a meeting.

If I wanted to attract non-sales people and the headline was:

A HAPPY NEW CAREER

or

IF YOU WERE BORN BETWEEN . . .

Then the copy was different:

If you are looking for a new career and are between 25 and 45 years of age, this may be the opportunity you have been looking for.

You may not have considered a career in sales but when you realize that every salesman earning over £20,000 per year was completely inexperienced when he applied for his first sales job, you will see that the same opportunity is open to you.

We are a company that not only recognizes the importance of the sales force and respects and rewards them accordingly but we welcome intelligent, ambitious but inexperienced applicants because we give full sales training.

We pay a generous salary plus commission and bonus and provide a company car that can be used for unlimited family motoring. Pension, BUPA and four weeks paid holiday are all part of the package. Opportunities for promotion into management are real after one year of service. What do we ask in return?

Something we all share, 100 per cent loyalty, enthusiasm, and the determination needed to make our company the most successful company in our industry.

If you would like to be one of us phone . . .

I have used dozens of advertisements over the years. They were all variations on the same theme which was:

1. This is an advertisement you should read.
2. This is the type of person we are looking for.
3. These are the wonderful opportunities we offer.

Some of you may be thinking 'it's easy to recruit the "right people" if you can offer a high salary, car, commission, bonus, promotion opportunities etc. etc.' I respond in two ways:

1. The object of the advertisement is to get as many suitable applicants as possible to apply.

2. You will not build a loyal controllable sales force unless they are salaried (even if the salary is very low) and high earning, for above-average performance.

Methods of remuneration are discussed in Chapter 15 and this is a chapter worth reading. There is no doubt that a crucial factor in the success or failure of a sales force is the manner in which they are remunerated.

Let me give you one example.

When I joined Ansafone in 1969 the sales force were offering a 7-year rental agreement and a 3-year rental agreement. Although the annual rental of the 3-year agreement was 50 per cent higher than the annual rental for the 7-year agreement, it meant that the value of the 7-year contract was 7 years rental and the value of the 3-year contract was 3 x 1.5 years rental = 4.5 years rental.

Obviously, the sales force were paid a higher commission on a 7-year contract than they were on a 3-year contract because the 'secured rental value' was higher. I discovered that the length of the contract had little relevance to the total rental we received.

We supplied a good product and our after-sales service was beyond reproach due to the efficiency of the service department under the direction of Doug Weston, the Service Director. As a result of this excellent service the 3year contract customers continued for further periods of 3 years, so that whereas over a period of 7 years we received £7x from a 7-year contract customer, we received £10.5x from a 3-year contract customer over a period of 6 years.

As I have explained, at the time that I became aware of this situation the sales force were paid commission on the secured rental value of the contract. That was 7x on a 7-year rental agreement and 4.5x on a 3-year rental agreement. Therefore, the sales force were being encouraged to generate the least profitable business for the company.

I changed the method of remuneration so that the salesmen were paid on the annual rental value of the contract and consequently they received 50 per cent more commission for selling a 3-year agreement than they did for selling a 7-year agreement.

This change in the method of remuneration for salesmen triggered what was probably the most important influence on Ansafone's profitability. This was at a time when inflation started to take off and we were locked into 7-year fixed rental contracts. A conventional price rise of 50 per cent was out of the question, neither the sales force nor the public would have accepted it, but this was what was achieved quite painlessly by switching the sales force from 7-year to 3-year contracts, by changing their method of remuneration.

If you cannot offer an attractive contract of employment to the applicants you attract from your advertising, I suggest you look at your whole business strategy very objectively, because it may be impossible for you to build a healthy, profitable sales force.

If the advertisement works you are going to have a lot of people – 20 to 200 – telephoning you, and you have to be very well organized to cope with 200 telephone calls.

Again I sense that some of you may be thinking 'why telephone calls, why not letters that we can evaluate in our own time?'

There is absolutely no doubt that if you are advertising for the head of the nuclear physics department, a telephone call for an interview would be totally inappropriate; you need written applications.

But if you are recruiting salesmen you must understand the type of person who will be successful. He is not prepared to take *no* for an answer, he wants to close the sale and if he cannot, he will look for another closing situation.

I found that if I interviewed a 'hot prospect' I had to get him on board within four days, before he had been offered a job by someone else.

Although the recruitment process was very fast it was also very thorough. If the advertisement appeared on a Tuesday it would be possible for someone to respond on Tuesday or Wednesday. They may be working during the day or they may be out of work. I was offering a company car, so they may not have a car.

The venue for the interview therefore had to be accessible to people without a car, and the hours during which interviews could be given had to be long enough to enable applicants in work to come after hours. I normally interviewed in a hotel in the centre of the main town in the territory or in the interview rooms which job centres will normally make available. The times stated in the advertisement were normally 9 a.m. to 8 p.m.

With Gross Cash Registers and Ansafone I normally let the secretaries answer the telephone and make first interview appointments at fifteen-minute intervals.

Obviously some applicants did not turn up but this gave the managers a chance of meeting every serious applicant and deciding if they felt they should be seen again.

In recent years I have been recruiting salesmen who have to make telephone appointments with the Chief Executives of most of our major institutions, and their telephone manner and technique are therefore among the most important qualities they must possess. I have therefore answered the telephone myself, to react (as if I were a prospect) to the applicant's telephone manner.

But whether I answer the telephone myself or have the secretaries answer it, the object is to get as many applicants as possible in for an interview as quickly as possible.

I find it very difficult to assess people's ability from a written application – I like to see them or talk to them.

I never cease to be amazed by the difference between the 'real man' and the CV which has been written by a professional CV agency. This raises a most important issue.

Do we really know whom we are recruiting?

There is absolutely no doubt that anyone going for an interview will present an exaggerated portrait of his own excellence. He may even produce glowing references.

The object of the recruitment interviews must be to try to find and evaluate the real applicant.

I do not believe you can do this by the inquisitorial techniques of 'sit him on a low chair with the light in his eyes. '

I do not even favour having a desk between me and the applicant even if this means the light is in *my* eyes.

I do not believe in management by domination. I believe the role of the successful manager is to bring out the best in his staff and this is seldom achieved by domination.

I find the ideal setting for interviews is a well furnished and comfortable office or hotel bedroom with two or three comfortable chairs and a coffee table.

The applicant should be greeted warmly, his coat taken, and you should invite him to sit in a particular chair where you can observe him naturally, not staring into the light or with his back to the light.

He should be told that this is an initial, informal exchange of information when you can ask him about his career to date and he can ask about the position to be filled.

The applicant should have completed an application form prior to the interview and the information recorded on the application form can then form the foundation upon which you will conduct a planned interview. On page 90 there is a sample application form for salesmen which has been especially designed (by me) to give us the information we need to evaluate both experienced salesmen and the applicant with no previous sales experience.

Part One gives us a profile of the applicant and highlights three danger areas:

1. Has he a stable home life?
2. Does he really need to work hard or has he an alternative income?
3. Is he likely to lose his driving licence?

It also gives us enough information to open up a friendly, relaxing conversation with the applicant. *Do not forget* we want to find out what the applicant is really like under the skin.

Initially the questions should be designed to relax him about his hobbies, his home life, etc.

Then if the applicant has been a salesman, the interview should be concerned solely with establishing how successful he has been. If he has been selling any speciality products or service, e.g. insurance, double-glazing, vending machines, or copiers, we must assume that he will do just as well or just as badly with us.

If he has not been in the top 50 per cent of the sales force he wants to leave, forget him. Tell him frankly that if he is not selling his present product easily he would not find your product any easier to sell, so 'thanks for coming but there is little point in meeting again.'

I cannot stress too strongly the simple test when interviewing salesmen. 'Have they been in the top 50 per cent of the sales force with previous employers?' If not, forget them. This test eliminates the possibility that the product was overpriced or under-engineered, or badly serviced, or ahead of its time. It measures the applicant's performance against his peers, salesmen who are selling the same product.

It is much more difficult to evaluate people who have never sold before but, knowing the type of person who could succeed, if he has the talent, we can at least eliminate many applicants by checking if they have the qualities that every salesman needs and also that they do not have those qualities that would make them a bad bet.

We have to try to find the 'real man', so with the inexperienced applicant it is more important than ever that we relax him.

I start off by finding something we have in common. It is amazing how rare it is for me to fail in finding a common bond between myself and the applicant.

I look at every entry on the application form and I usually find that I have:

(a) A knowledge of one of the places he has lived or worked in.
(b) A knowledge of one of the companies he has worked for.
(c) A knowledge of the industry in which he has been employed.
(d) A common hobby.
(e) Children of the same age, etc.

I like to start there. I want to find the 'real man'. Forget about the interview, forget about the CV and the testimonial letters.

I do not mean to imply that his previous career history and the testimonial letters are not important – they are – but they are the image that the applicant wishes to project in the mistaken belief that even if he is not really right for the job, it is better to be selected and fail than to be rejected. After all, are we not taught that it is better to have loved and lost than never to have loved at all?

Sadly, previous employers, family and friends will all conspire to help an applicant get a job for which he is not suited. They will write references which say:

'Not suited to our type of selling' – this means he cannot sell.

'Due to reorganization' – this means, we sacked him and his boss because neither of them could sell.

'Redundant' – this means he cannot sell.

'Ability fair, integrity excellent' – this means he cannot sell.

We therefore have to accept that the overall impression we get from both an applicant who has been selling before, and also his previous employers, will be better than he really is, so if in doubt about his real ability do not hire him.

It is purely wishful thinking to think that we are so gifted in sales training that we can turn a failure into a success. Obviously we may be able to on rare occasions but the odds are stacked against us.

Family and friends are even more devious. They will do anything to help their loved one secure employment, so character references must be treated with a great deal of circumspection.

I remember particularly a salesman I engaged at Gross Cash Registers, who was not only a 'good salesman' as confirmed by previous employers, but was also a man of 'good character' as confirmed by the major of the local Salvation Army citadel in Lancashire. When I spoke to the major, to check his references, I was told that Wilson, the applicant, had been an alcoholic but that was now behind him.

He proved to be an excellent salesman and was indeed a member of the Salvation Army, as was his wife. She had been a member long enough to qualify for the uniform, whereas he was still working towards qualification, his personal goal in life.

After a couple of months he went missing. He failed to report to the office and he, the company van, and full complement of stock could not be traced. Needless to say, his wife was distraught and we were genuinely concerned.

It was ten days later that the telephone rang in my office in Brighton.

'It's reception here, Mr Adams, there's a Mr Wilson to see you.'

Although it seemed improbable, I knew he must be the missing salesman.

'Send him up,' I said.

Sure enough, it was Wilson.

He was smartly dressed, clean, clear-eyed, just as he had been when I engaged him.

He didn't wait for me to say anything. He dived in, head first.

'I've been on a drinking bout,' he said, 'I don't expect you to understand or sympathize, in fact the only reason I am here is to thank you for giving me the chance to work for you even when you knew that I was an alcoholic, and to return to you, in good condition, the company van and all my stock.'

'Well, where do you go from here?' I asked.

'I don't know,' he said, 'but one thing I do know, I've learned my lesson. Not only have I let you down and lost the job you gave me, knowing I was an alcoholic, but I lost my chance of getting "the uniform". I'll never drink again as long as I live.'

'Does your wife know you're here?' I asked.

'No,' he said.

I buzzed my secretary on the intercom. 'Get me Mrs Wilson on the telephone will you, Joan.'

We sat in silence with our own thoughts.

Suddenly the telephone rang. I picked it up to hear Joan say 'Mrs Wilson on the line for you.' 'Hello, Mrs Wilson, this is Tony Adams from Gross Cash Registers.'

'Oh, hello, Mr Adams, I'm afraid I haven't any news for you, John is still missing,' she said, obviously under tremendous strain.

'It's all right, Mrs Wilson. John is with me, he is all right and ready to come home.'

'Oh, thank God!' she said. 'What can I say, I'm so sorry he has let you down. I don't know what we will do now but the Lord will provide. Can I speak to him?'

'Of course, ' I said .

I handed the telephone over to John Wilson and left the office to give him the chance to talk to his wife in private.

I watched through the glass partition and thought, 'there but for the Grace of God goes any one of us'.

I saw him put the telephone back on its rest, gave him a few moments to collect his thoughts, and went back into my office.

'Well, I'll be going,' he said. 'I can't thank you enough and I can't apologize enough for letting you down, but I'll tell you one thing, I'll never drink again as long as I live, so help me God.'

'Sit down,' I said.

'So you really mean it?' I asked. 'Do you really mean that this has given you the determination to stay teetotal for the rest of your life?'

'I do,' he said, 'what is more, I'm going to ask the Major if I can start all over again to qualify for the "uniform".'

He put his hand in his pocket, pulled out the keys of his van and put them on my desk.

'Here are the keys,' he said. 'Would you like to come down and check my stock?'

'Keep the keys,' I said. 'Drive your van home and get out to work tomorrow and prove to us all that you have kicked the habit for good.'

I can't describe the effect this had on him. I can only say that he drove away, fired with a new enthusiasm to prove that the Lord would help him to overcome his alcoholism and to repay me for my trust in him. Almost as if nothing had happened, the sales came rolling in the next week and the week after.

The week after that he went missing again.

5

Recruitment – fine tuning of selection

Recruiting salesmen is always a hit and miss business.

It is so different from recruiting any other type of employee because you cannot really give them an aptitude test.

If you are recruiting a new secretary you can establish their familiarity with the relevant information technology systems, provide them with some tasks, and judge their efficiency by the speed, accuracy and layout of the documents they produce.

Salesmen with a proven record of achievement are seldom on the labour market. They stay with their present employers where they have the security of continuing success or they look around for a sales management appointment if promotion opportunities do not present themselves 'in house'. So we are trying to evaluate people with no track record, for the most part.

We all know that recruitment is an expensive process and unsuccessful recruitment even more so. It is not just the cost of the advertisements, it is the cost of training and paying a salesman for many weeks.

The most serious 'cost' of unsuccessful recruitment is the loss of business from that territory and the loss of time that can never be replaced, so I have always been very conscious of the need to eliminate wrong selection as far as possible.

At Ansafone we had about a 50 per cent success rate when recruiting 'non-salesmen' and this was very costly. I was, in fact, sitting at my desk, trying to work out how much it cost us to recruit one successful salesman, when the telephone rang.

It was a firm of industrial psychologists introducing a process of psychological testing of job applicants to eliminate the risk of engaging someone who is not suited to the job.

I was very receptive to the idea but I had a number of reservations. It was not uncommon for us to have 200 applicants for one vacant territory (and still we got it wrong). So the cost of testing 200 applicants would make the whole process unviable. You could well argue that if it ensured that we recruited a successful applicant every time, it would be viable because we would eliminate the real problem of vacant or unproductive territories.

The trouble was, I did not know if it worked.

The test consisted of a sixteen-page questionnaire, most of which was in the form of multiple choices:

'Would you rather be a painter, a chemist, a violinist, a chiropodist, or a sailor?'

A few pages later there was another question:

'Would you rather be a sculptor, a pharmacist, a trumpeter, a physiotherapist, or a marine?'

Not only did I not know if it worked, I just could not see how we could get all 200 applicants to fill out this sixteen-page form and then wait a week or more for the result before knowing if they had qualified for an interview. The cost was also prohibitive.

Although the objections, or should I call them reservations, were considerable, I decided to employ these psychologists to see what they could do.

I adopted an unconventional approach. Instead of letting them test applicants *before* appointment, I decided to use my standard procedure of recruitment, which was only 50 per cent successful, and then *after* they had been appointed, on their first day in the induction training course I gave them the complete industrial psychologists' sixteen-page test.

I made it quite clear to them that their future career and prospects of promotion would not be affected by the results of the test. I also made it quite clear to them that it was the psychological test that was on trial, not them.

Whether they believed me or not they completed the questionnaire and I sent them off for evaluation.

Naturally I considered carefully whether the method of assessment I was using was valid. I had eliminated 90 per cent of all applicants before giving the psychologists a chance to test them. Suppose I had eliminated all the truly talented applicants and I was giving the analysts only the dross to analyse?

I thought long and hard about this because we all know that there are lies, damned lies, and statistics.

I was finally satisfied that the experiment I was conducting was valid because I was giving the psychologists some 200 people to test for sales and sales management aptitudes. It did not matter how they had been selected. If I had selected well, they should confirm this. If I had selected badly this should confirm it.

The only thing I did know, as a control if you like, was that if I recruited 100 people I was right 50 per cent of the time and wrong 50 per cent of the time.

The psychologists sent me their reports in due time and I paid them each time we recruited, until we had recruited and tested 200 men. I was not concerned with whether they agreed with me or not, I was concerned with their degree of success. They had to commit themselves with every salesman before he had been out on the road and they proved to be absolutely right 50 per cent of the time and wrong 50 per cent of the time, based on their assessment and the salesman's achievement over the first thirteen weeks!

Obviously they could not help me, but I had to find a way of improving my method of recruitment. If 50 per cent of my selections were right and 50 per cent wrong I might just as well toss a dice or flip a coin.

It was at about that time that Walt Disney's *Jungle Book* was being televised and by chance I heard the rich and fruity voice of Phil Harris emanating from the mouth of a great big bear: 'You simply got to accentuate the positive, eliminate the negative, latch on to the affirmative, and don't mess with Mr In-between'.

I could never have defined the recruitment selection process more succinctly had I pored over my typewriter for months.

There was one problem.

I could not 'accentuate the positive' because I knew that the positive was the talent that successful salesmen possess, the talent that cannot be recognized until it has manifested itself.

So I condensed the lyric:

'You simply got to eliminate the negative and don't mess with Mr In-between.'

I could look at those dozens, nay, I blush, hundreds of salesmen I, or we, had employed over the years, who had failed, and conduct a post mortem to establish beyond reasonable doubt the cause of failure. It was valuable to learn that many of the failures failed due to factors other than lack of sales ability.

If you have a big enough sample to analyse you come up with some pretty conclusive conclusions. For instance, if you recruit 500 people between the ages of 20 and 40, and no one under the age of 23 is successful, you conclude that it is a bad commercial risk to employ anyone under the age of 23. True?

If you employ fifty wives or husbands of high-earning husbands or wives and none of them succeeds, you will conclude that it is a bad commercial risk to employ someone who is not the major breadwinner. Right?

But I found there were some far more subtle indicators.

I found that if someone failed to complete the job application form in detail he was a bad risk.

So I built a register of negatives to be eliminated until I was able to define company recruitment policy in detail. I was able to state, as a fact, that every unsuccessful recruit fell into one or more of the following categories, but no successful recruit fell into any of the category A or more than one category B classification.

Category A

1. Under 22 years of age.
2. Frequent changes of employment without a career pattern emerging.
3. Housewife with young children.
4. One-parent family with young children.
5. Had been run-of-the-mill salesman for some years.
6. Had two current endorsements on his driving licence.

Category B

1. No 'O' level examination passes.
2.   Not the main breadwinner in the family.
3. Reluctance to complete the application form in detail.
4. Unstable marital state.
5. Left previous employment without a job to go to.
6. Had held speciality sales job before but held it for less than a year.
7. Had another source of income.
8. Too highly qualified or was in too senior management at previous employment.

I was at this time controlling a large sales force and I was not personally responsible for the final selection of any applicant, and therefore, to minimize errors of judgement, I made it known that we would not recruit any applicant with any category A quality or any applicant with any two category B qualities.

You may wonder how I can justify this process of elimination and I reply: 'Because of the statistical evidence,' but never mind the facts, what are the reasons?

A.1   Under 22 years of age

If you have read *The Secrets of Successful Selling* you will know that the difference between success and failure in selling is 'confidence'. The word 'confidence' has many meanings but in this context it means, more than anything, that the buyer must have confidence in the salesman's ability to give him good advice. A salesman of 21 years of age or less is fighting an uphill battle because, let us face it, he has very little business experience, if any. How can a mature businessman have confidence in his advice?

A.2   Frequent changes in employment without a career pattern emerging

It does not matter what new project you undertake, it takes time and persistence to master the new skills required. I knew that frequent changes in employment meant that the applicant had found it difficult to adapt and had run away from problems rather than face up to them. It also indicated lack of pride in achievement.

I have some first-class salesmen with me now who found it very difficult to adapt to a new product, a new method of working. They could have thrown in the sponge after a few weeks and looked for something different. They did not. They had the guts, the stickability, the determination, the pride, that would not let them fail in an arena where others were succeeding, and, of course, they are now successful. They are the people I want to recruit, not the lily-livered drifters.

A.3   Housewives with young children

I recognize that it is very natural, right, and proper for an intelligent woman with children to look for a job that is mentally stimulating. I know, from my own experience, that face-to-face with a prospect, women are as effective as men. But selling is not a 9 to 4 occupation, neither is it one that can take second place to family responsibilities.

I am not saying that a woman's place is in the home. I am not saying a man's place is in the home. I am saying that if you are recruiting salesmen, a married woman with young children is a bad bet. It may not be justice but it is a fact.

School holidays, children's illnesses, dentist appointments, shopping – all manner of distractions, reduce her effectiveness during the week, and it is also difficult for her to keep evening and weekend appointments, let alone spend five days away at an exhibition or travel abroad for export business.

I have found women without school-age children very effective.

A.4   One-parent families

It is even more difficult for the one-parent family to cope than it is for the housewife, for the housewife usually has the help of her husband. The one-parent family relies on friends, relatives, neighbours, employed help, all of whom have responsibilities of their own which they will put before the single parent's problems. I was a single parent for four years and I know how difficult it is.

A.5   Has been a run-of-the-mill salesman for some years

This was virtually positive proof that he would be a run-of-the-mill salesman with us and I could not afford to have a territory tied up with a run-of-the-mill salesman. I knew that unless a salesman had been well up in the top half of his previous employer's sales force, he would not be in the top half of ours.

A.6 Two current endorsements on his driving licence

At the time I laid down these standards you lost your driving licence for a year if you had three current endorsements. Today disqualification is decided by the number of points you have managed to accumulate. It is bad management to recruit and train a salesman who could lose his licence by committing one more offence. If he has got that close to disqualification he is either a dreadful or dangerous driver or he has not got the common sense to keep his eye on his rear-view mirror. Whatever the cause, it is unlikely that he will become an alert paragon of virtue overnight, and the chances are that within six months of recruitment he will lose his driving licence.

I made it quite clear to my management team that they were not to recruit any applicant with any one of the category A characteristics. Category B was different.

Some people with a category B characteristic had been successful in the past but no one, I repeat no one, had been successful with two category B characteristics.

B.1 No 'O' level examinations passed

Although we cannot define intelligence accurately, or measure its value in selling, I discovered that the overwhelming majority of our successful salesmen did fairly well at school. The few graduates that I was able to recruit did exceptionally well.

To be successful with us it was necessary to learn and remember a great deal of information and to act as a business adviser, and if an applicant had not managed to pass a single 'O' level examination there was real doubt about his ability to learn and remember information. There may be extenuating circumstances such as living abroad, or illness during childhood, but an applicant with a good academic record must be preferred.

Of course, there is always the exception to the rule.

At Gross Cash Registers one of the managers recruited a huge

Irishman, predictably called Patrick Murphy. He was 6 feet 3 inches tall and tipped the scale at 17 stone. He was not fat, he was just *big*, with goalkeeper's hands. At that time we were still selling the old-fashioned 'press down' cash registers with two rows of keys to record pounds, shillings, and pence. They were large mechanical devices weighing some ninety pounds. He could put his giant fingers under the keys of one of these ninety-pound cash registers, lift it from the floor and put it gently down on the shopkeeper's counter, exactly where he wanted it. We called him the 'Gentle Giant'. He had been through the seven-day induction training course; he had been told about features and benefits and buying signals and closing techniques, but he could not be bothered with all that; he had kissed the Blarney Stone.

'Just look at that,' he would say, once he had placed the cash register on the counter. 'Doesn't that just do something to you?'

'Come round here where I am standing and see how the sun shines off the grey and the blue. Sure, it's like an April morning, so it is.'

'Doesn't it do something to your shop now?'

'Doesn't it make it look a different place, altogether?'

'Can't you see the customers saying, "That's a gorgeous till you've got there Mr Miller, you must be doing well now, mustn't you? We're pleased for you. The shop would never be the same again without it".'

'And it does do something for the shop doesn't it?'

Not only could he charm the birds off the trees, he let nothing stop him from doing an honest day's work. One day his car broke down and, whereas a normal, *intelligent* salesman would accept the inevitable and miss a day's selling, he picked up two ninety-pound demonstration machines, one in each hand, and went to work on the bus.

I never found another Gentle Giant. Most of the applicants with poor academic achievements were, as you would expect, slow to learn and unable to think on their feet.

B.2 *Not the main breadwinner in the family*

You may think this is the same as housewives with young children, but it is not.

This week I have been interviewing applicants for a sales appointment. I have been looking for mature people with management experience that would enable them to converse with directors of large companies as equals, without tugging the forelock. One applicant impressed me. He had a public school education, had obtained a pass degree in law at London University and, after four years in the army as a junior officer, had worked his way up the commercial ladder from dogsbody to general manager. Like so many others he had been made redundant, and at the age of 38 was prepared to start again, as a salesman, and work his way up. I short-listed him and asked him back for a second interview.

He telephoned the office on the day before the second interview to say that he could not attend because his wife, who is a solicitor, had to be in court and he had to stay at home to look after the children.

A few years ago we recruited the husband of an up-and coming TV soap opera actress. Within months he resigned to become her manager.

Recently I recruited a man whose wife has a prosperous ladies hairdressing 'salon'. He was distracted by the need to give the children a stable home life and fetch and carry for his wife.

In my experience the 'breadwinner' in a partnership is the only person to recruit.

B.3 Reluctance to complete the application form in detail

Since laying down these standards several years ago I have seriously considered upgrading this characteristic to category A.

Every successful applicant I know is proud to record full details of his career and provide dates, earnings, and references. The applicants that miss out some of their less glamorous episodes or who are coy about their earnings usually have good cause to be. There is a great divide between the man who has nothing to hide and the man who has something to hide.

Never forget that when you are reading application forms there are two particularly important areas to watch.

The first and most important is start and finish dates for each employment. If these dates do not provide a continuous employment history, forget it. It does not necessarily mean that the applicant has been in jail but it does mean that there are periods in his life that he would rather forget probably periods of failure or unemployment.

The second is the income progression. I am not interested in people who are on the way down. I want to see an earnings progression, and people who leave the earnings column blank do not have this progression. If they had, they would be proud to record it on the application form.

Some excellent applicants have been made redundant for reasons which are not a reflection on their ability and, rather than be unemployed, take up employment at a salary or commission level which is below what they had enjoyed previously. These honest, applicants will declare this information freely, without cross-examination, so view, with suspicion, anyone. who does not declare his income on a job application form.

B.4   Marital status

Once upon a time people were either married or single, and one could consider whether it would be better to employ a single person who was mobile or a married person with a sense of responsibility.

The majority of applicants still fall into these two categories, but also some are happy to tell me that their wives are 'common law wives' or 'partners'.

Unmarried partners are becoming more stable than they used to be, and although I am an old-fashioned heterosexual I must confess that two of the best salesmen I have ever employed, not only lived together but bought their house in joint names.

The important thing to establish is whether the relationship is stable, and although you cannot ask the question directly and would not get an honest answer if you did, you can, during the interview, get a pretty good picture by talking about the family, the hobbies, the partner's occupation, and so on.

My analysis of the failures had provided me with overwhelming evidence that an unstable home life made the applicant a very bad risk. He or she was likely to spend a lot of time sorting out emotional problems and quite likely to disappear, like Adam to his own Garden of Eden.

B.5 Left previous employment without another job to go to

There have been very few occasions in my life when I have felt like telling my boss where to put his job, but on those few occasions I have held my peace, knowing that it is far more difficult to obtain employment when you are unemployed and in need of a job than it is when you are in employment.

The man who resigns with no new job to go to is either very hot-headed or very foolish. 99 per cent of the people who leave their employment without having a better job to go to have either been sacked or have resigned to avoid dismissal.

On the other hand, there are regrettably tens of thousands of able, intelligent, and industrious people on the labour market today who have been made redundant due to the technological revolution we are going through or due to incompetent management.

If an applicant is unemployed it is essential to establish, through careful questioning, the reason for his being unemployed.

There is a double problem. If he was not made redundant but resigned, he may be very hot-headed or foolish. If, on the other hand, he was made redundant he may well take any job offered to pay the rent, even if it is not what he is really looking for. There is a very real risk he will have several irons in the fire, and after one or two weeks of training he will resign to accept 'a better job' that has now been offered him.

It has happened to me more than once. I have even had an induction training course interrupted in mid-week by a telephone call for one of the trainees, which was a job offer!

Be careful about the unemployed!

B.6   Has held a speciality sales job before but has held it for less than a year

I have sold seven different speciality products or services over a period of thirty-four years. They have ranged from encyclopaedias to cash registers to telecommunication consultancy. If you can sell one, you can sell them all.

If a salesman works for one successful company, but has given it up because he did not like it or could not do it, there is virtually no chance that he will succeed with another product or service. I had a few exceptions, so this was a category B characteristic.

B. 7   Has another source of income

I do not say that all salesmen are motivated only by money and that if they have another source of income they will not work. I have never been motivated by money; I have been motivated by the need to excel, to be successful at everything I have undertaken. You could say that it is more important for me to earn the respect of my peers than to 'make money'. Fortunately for me, in a selling environment the two are inseparable. If you succeed in selling you earn both money and respect.

I am not too worried about the man who has a rich wife. Often this acts as an additional incentive for him to prove himself. I am worried about the man who earns money from a hobby or sideline.

The fact that he has another interest will affect him in two ways. First, there will not be the same financial incentive for him to give his 'all' to the job and, second, there will be another business interest to which he will devote constructive thinking time which should be devoted to us.

Sometimes this problem is closely linked to B.2, 'Not the main breadwinner in the family', although at the time of recruitment this was not the case.

I remember particularly an excellent salesman whose wife had a small business selling raffle tickets and other low value items to

Working Men's Clubs, Rotary Clubs, and so on, so that they could engage in fund raising activities. It seemed harmless enough but gradually the range of products grew, business grew to the point where it was no longer a case of giving his wife a hand in the evenings but 'which activity is most profitable?' He left to join his wife in the business.

Another classic case was the man in Cornwall whose wife ran a boarding house. Did I say his wife ran a boarding house? *They* ran a boarding house during the summer months and *he* needed a job in the winter. Of course there are marginal cases. You could argue that because I spend some of my time writing and thereby earn 'another source of income' I should not be employed as a salesman, and you would be right because the next B characteristic is:

B.8   Too highly qualified or was in too senior management at previous employment

Nowadays this has to be viewed in conjunction with the age of the applicant.

So many people are made redundant these days that there is a permanent reservoir of unemployed salesmen, sales managers, sales directors, marketing directors, all on the labour market, looking for a job that will enable them to meet the mortgage payments and restore their self respect.

Although you are considered too young to be Prime Minister of England if you are under 50, and can be re-elected as President of the United States if you are over 70, you are 'over the hill' at 40 as a salesman or sales manager. Ludicrous but true.

I say ludicrous but maybe it is not. If you are over 40 you were not educated in the binary code, new maths, WP, LAN, IT era. You are frightened at the sight of a computer keyboard.

You were taught that 12 pennies = 1 shilling, 112 lb = 1 cwt, and 7 x 8 = 56, and if you begin a letter 'Dear Sir' you must end it 'Yours truly'.

There is a generation gap and there is no point in denying it.

As is always the case, the extremes are easy to identify.

If you have an application from a 28-year-old BSc., Ph. D graduate of Harvard Business School applying for a job as salesman on a low salary, high commission package, he is simply looking for a company car and beer money (or is it gin-and-tonic money?) to tide him over until he meets someone who will give his talents the respect that they deserve.

If, on the other hand, you have an application from a 50year-old man who has been a successful salesman, sales manager, and sales director who was made redundant six months ago, it is a different matter altogether. He has probably resigned himself to the fact that he is not going to be offered a job as sales director, no matter how often he applies, and he must therefore settle for the humiliation of the dole or start all over again as a salesman, using the skills he has acquired over the years to earn a good living and, what is perhaps more important to him, *respect*.

When I was recruiting for large, growing sales forces I was looking for lean and hungry young men with careers to build, windmills to tilt at. I was not interested in yesterday's man. And I was right.

It needed potential managers – hungry salesmen, but maybe I should have spread my net wider, for now I have a sales force of highly successful salesmen who have been turned down by the up and coming, dynamic sales forces purely on account of their age.

Is that not incredible?

The young man will not be content to work as a salesman for long, and will therefore job hunt if there is not an offer of promotion within a few months of appointment.

The highly qualified (in sales terms) 50-year-old will be grateful and loyal to the employer who allows him to exercise his sales skills, to earn a good living, and to re-establish himself as a successful member of his own local community.

So perhaps I should re-write the B.8 characteristic as 'Too highly qualified *young man* in senior management at previous employment'. As I say, I am currently employing some first-class 'over 40' salesmen.

Their backgrounds vary dramatically. One is an extrovert marketing man who describes himself as a stage door Johnny who married the star of the show. Another is a carpet bagger who traded in Nigeria; need I say more. Another was a commodity dealer, another a computer salesman, a fifth was a British Leyland main agent, and a sixth was – well what does it matter what the sixth one was, or the seventh. What matters is, if you are looking for restructuring you must recruit energetic young men who will be the management material for the years to come.

If you are not looking for growth, which is rather different from re-structuring, redundant 50-year-olds may well prove to be the most effective, loyal, hardworking salesmen you can recruit.

6

Recruitment – final selection

A friend of mine recently decided to build a utility room on the back of his house as an extension to the kitchen. It was nothing very grand, about two metres wide and three metres long, but room enough for a sink and double drainer, the washing machine, tumble drier, and a deep freeze.

He had a friend who was an architect so it was not difficult for him to get planning permission and detailed drawings that would enable him to get accurate estimates for the building work. Rather than engage a builder, who would tender for the whole job, he decided to save money and employ direct labour, a builder to build the shell, including the roof, door, and window, an electrician to do the wiring, a plumber to do the plumbing, and a plasterer to plaster the walls and ceiling. He reckoned he could decorate it himself and lay the floor tiles.

He is a very capable person, not only with his hands but also as an organizer. Not only did he obtain competitive tenders for each phase of the operation, he established how many days each tradesman would need and the order in which they had to work. He even checked on the availability of materials to ensure shortages would not hold up progress.

Those of you familiar with critical path analysis will recognize this exercise as a very simple problem to solve and so it proved to be.

He accepted the most favourable quotations and gave each of the tradesmen the date on which they should start and the date by which they were required to complete their stage of the construction programme.

Only one thing went wrong, *not one of the tradesmen turned up*.

If you are not very careful, arranging and conducting interviews can be very much the same. If you do not accept an estimate from an electrician immediately it is highly likely that he has accepted enough work to keep him busy for the next six months while you have been deciding which tender to accept.

In the same way if, after you have completed all your first interviews over a period of several days, you write to those you have short-listed inviting them to attend a second interview you may well find that a number of them do not turn up.

To prevent this happening you must first make sure that the whole recruitment process is condensed into as short a time span as decently possible and, second, you must do everything you can to make each applicant want to be successful in his application. You remember my saying that if something is in short supply it is more highly valued? Remember the Melbourne factory workers having only thirty minutes in which to get drunk? Well, so it is with recruitment.

At the first interview you must give the impression that the job you are offering is highly prized. A unique opportunity for which a very large number of applicants are competing. Although you should be eliminating all the A and 2B type applicants and many other unsuitables, you must not let the ones you like feel that it is they who hold the reins, they who will decide whether or not they work for you, for if you allow this to happen not only will you have lost control of the recruitment process, you will have diminished the job on offer, not only now but in the future.

If you feel you are interviewing a 'winner', present the job in the most favourable light possible within the time constraints of the first interview and then don't say 'Well, how does it sound to you? Do you think you would enjoy working with us?' for by so doing you have lost control.

By contrast say 'As you will appreciate, I shall be selecting a short list of applicants that I shall invite back for a second interview. Would you telephone me tomorrow between 5 and 6 p.m. and I shall then be able to tell you if you are on the short list'.

This acts as a third screening process. The first screen was getting the right people to apply to the advertisement and come to the interview, the second was on short listing, the third is getting rid of those 'short-listed' applicants who are not interested in us.

Those applicants who do telephone back as requested have shown genuine interest and are either told 'Sorry, you are not on the short list', with the blow being softened by 'So many applicants with similar successful previous experience', or 'Yes, you are on the short list and I would like you to come for a second interview with our Mr . . . on . . . at . . . '. Here is another test of the applicant's sincerity; if he really wants the job he will come when we want to see him even if he has to reschedule appointments. Only if the reason given for being unable to attend at that time and date is acceptable to *you*, e.g. 'I am getting married on that day' should you *readily* agree to another time and day and then only if you are very keen to recruit him.

Not only is a second interview invariably necessary to cover all the detail that must be covered before a final decision could be reached by either side, it is also necessary to enable both parties to get a true picture of each other in a more relaxed atmosphere than is possible in hurried first interviews.

Furthermore, it is my view that unless we are talking about a one-man business there should always be two different interviewers who will inevitably see the applicant in a different light and who will therefore, together, be able to reach a more balanced, less biased, view of the applicant. We all tend to recruit clones and this must be tempered by an unbiased opinion.

I have always regarded it as essential for the manager who has to train and manage that salesman to have the final say on who is recruited. For a third party, be it a personnel manager or general sales manager to say 'Here is your new salesman – make him succeed' is totally unreasonable. I have therefore always regarded first interviews as a mechanical screening process which should not encroach upon the branch sales manager's valuable time, working with his men in the field. He should be presented with two, three, or four short-listed applicants from which he can make his final selection or, if he has no faith in any of them, reject them all.

If the first interviews have been conducted by his immediate superior, which I have always favoured, then I think it is a good idea for them both to be. present at the second interviews, with the branch sales manager 'in the chair' conducting the interview, and his boss observing and taking part as and when he feels it appropriate.

An hour should be allowed for each interview, and the branch manager should do all he can to make the applicant relaxed, for we want to find out what the man is really like.

He should be treated like a potential customer because that is what he is. We want to sell him the company and we want him to 'buy'. This enables us at the end of the day to choose which applicant *we* want to recruit because they all want the job.

Offer to take his coat, offer him coffee, invite him to smoke, if he does, even if it gets up your nose.

Using his application form, draw him out and if you find any discrepancies between the notes made on the form at the first interview and what he tells you now, draw him out some more. All the while you should be showing interest in him and at the same time evaluating him and ensuring there are no category A or B qualities that have not been disclosed.

Obviously you are going to assess the successful salesman differently from the inexperienced applicant.

The successful salesman

You must satisfy yourself that he really is (a) successful and (b) a salesman.

(a) By far the best way to measure a salesman's success is by way of his earnings. The application form will show you what his earnings have been not only over the last three months but over the final three months of each previous employment expressed as salary and commission.

   You can also ask if he has his commission sheets or sales records with him.

   Has he taken part in any sales competitions? How did he fare?

(b) The best way to tell if he is a salesman is to ask him to sell you the product or service he is selling at the moment, to treat you as a prospect. Obviously, he may be without his sales kit but you will get a jolly good idea of how convincing he is. Ask him what closing techniques he uses. Ask him how he prospects. Ask him what his conversion ratio is.

You must be very firm with yourself and recruit no man with previous sales experience unless it is clearly proved that he is a successful salesman.

If he is a successful salesman, why is he changing jobs?

There could be many reasons, some of which are acceptable, but many that are not.

The most common is 'I am looking for more money'.

If he really is a successful salesman he should be earning a lot of money, so you must take what he says very seriously and go through his earnings month my month and relate this to performance. Compare with others in the same company. If you are satisfied that he really is an underpaid, successful salesman fine, but you must also be satisfied that he will earn more money with you, otherwise you will have the same problem with him in a few months' time.

You will very often find that he has been a successful salesman but that his earnings have dropped due to a fall in his level of sales in recent times. If this is the case you must find out why. If you cannot find a cause you must speak about this when you take up telephone references should you decide to recruit him.

Sometimes a drop in earnings is due to the second reason for leaving, 'I am looking for something more mentally stimulating'.

Very few salesmen can go on forever selling the same product without getting stale.

The successful salesman we are looking for could well get frustrated after a few years, and as soon as a salesman starts thinking about changing his job his sales start to decline. A new challenge, a new product, may well restore his enthusiasm.

Another legitimate reason for a successful salesman to be looking around is 'The company is failing'.

It is not unusual for salesmen with small companies to find that commission cheques do not arrive on time. There are many excellent salesmen who have broken into selling the hard way selling home improvements and who can see little future for themselves where they are, due to the instability of the company they work for.

Sometimes a successful salesman will say he is leaving because 'There are no opportunities for promotion'.

This in itself is a commendable reason for leaving. He is ambitious, and if you can genuinely offer him a chance of promotion within one or two years, and he accepts this timescale, he could be an excellent recruit. If, on the other hand, you are looking for a salesman to work a territory for many years to come and cannot genuinely offer him a superior remuneration package, you must face up to the fact that he will again be looking around for a job with more prospects before the year is out.

Very often a salesman will say he is leaving because 'I don't agree with the management'.

There is no way you can make a snap judgement on this one. It needs exploring in great detail. He may complain that when he joined his present company his territory was 'so big', but now 'it's only so big'.

If you plan to increase the size of your sales force you will have trouble with him unless you spell out your plans to him and this you may not want to do. Whenever I have had a salesman complain to me about an adjustment to his territory, I ask him how he got his territory in the first place.

He may complain that his manager takes all the best business off his territory. You need to know if this is a normal house account situation or is his manager stealing commission from him and, if so, why. It is dangerous to assume that the management is always right. Salesmen can have very genuine grievances against their management. You need to find out the truth.

Some salesmen leave because they were 'Unsuccessful in management'.

A fair percentage of salesmen who are promoted into management do not succeed. The demotion that follows is a traumatic experience for that manager and it is extremely difficult for him to revert to the rank of salesman among colleagues who were once under his control. It sometimes works, but not often.

Such an applicant can be an excellent salesman who has got the management bug out of his system and should be considered very seriously.

Naturally you have to be certain that he accepts that he is not cut out for management at this stage in his career, and that he is not really a manager at heart who is prepared to take a job as a salesman as a 'fill in' to tide him over until he can find a better job in management.

If you are interested in him it is then up to you to sell him the company.

Enthuse about the product.

Enthuse about the company.

Enthuse about the remuneration, even if the salary is low, enthuse about his high earnings potential.

Enthuse about the promotion prospects if they are there.

Get 'his side of the counter' so that he identifies with you, a successful branch manager.

Give him *all* the relevant factual information he needs to enable him to evaluate the job properly.

He should be told:

- Company background and history.
- Product range and features.
- Salary scales, including holiday and sickness entitlement.
- Commission and bonus package.
- Quotas and minimum standards of performance.

- These should be compared with average performance and the performance of the top salesmen.

Territory, shooting rights, house accounts, are all vital pieces of information for the experienced salesman and there should not be any misunderstandings when he joins, for that can be very demotivating.

If he is required to prospect for new business, make sure he understands that the job is not only converting enquiries.

If he still wants the job, he should be asked to telephone you at your office the following morning. This is the fourth filter.

If you find that his previous selling experience is not similar to the job you are offering, treat him as if he were an inexperienced applicant.

The inexperienced applicant

Hopefully, the first interview will have eliminated all the hopeless cases, the As and the Bs and the illiterates.

There is, however, one other category of applicant who is often a bad risk. He is the man with a great deal of energy and intelligence, who prefers to be independent and could not enjoy working as one of a team, conforming to company methods and routines. He may be self-employed.

It is extremely difficult to draw a line between the ideal applicant who, because of his strength of character, is successful but difficult to manage, and the man who is rebellious, but if there is a previous history which you learn from the interview or subsequently from previous employers of failure to conform to company procedures, then you can bet that he will not change.

The man who has the most demanding job in terms of effort, hours, and discomfort, but who has done it well and now seeks an even more demanding but rewarding challenge is the ideal applicant.

If you were selecting a team of men or women to accompany you on an expedition where each is dependent on the other, you would be looking for the same type of character.

You would not want someone who would decide to turn back half way. This may seem an over-dramatic way to see the task of recruiting salesmen, but if you think of the best salesmen you know you would find it difficult to imagine them turning back half way.

So, in our interview, we are evaluating the applicant on the basis of his behaviour in the past.

We must get him to *sell* us something he believes in, his particular sport, his favourite holiday resort, his home town or native country, whatever *he* believes in, to see if he 'comes alive', to see if he can get us to share his enthusiasm or at least accept that he is sincere. I can't think of any nasty, bad tempered, or argumentative successful salesmen, for good salesmen have a highly developed sense of empathy, and even if they disagree with someone they use tact and understanding to try to find a meeting of minds.

So, to summarize, although the applicant should have an attractive personality, this is not enough. There must be evidence of determination to succeed, coupled with empathy and enthusiasm. If you see these qualities in him, he should be given full information about the company and the appointment and be invited to ask questions.

He should be asked to telephone the office for a decision next day.

The short-listed applicants should then be evaluated carefully. If there is no one that the branch manager is really enthusiastic about, the senior manager may exercise his discretion on rare occasions and select someone he feels *will* be successful, but if neither the branch nor senior manager feels enthusiastic about any short-listed applicant then no one should be appointed and the recruitment procedure should be repeated.

Normally there will be a successful candidate.

It is not ethical to telephone his present employer until he has been offered the job and accepted it, but in the case of experienced salesmen *it is most important to speak to previous employers before a final decision is reached.*

If the applicant is currently employed, you should telephone as many previous employers as you can to get an accurate impression of his ability and integrity.

Do not recruit other firms' failures.

Thinking positively you can recognize the right man by his previous sales record and by talking to his previous immediate superior.

When the short-listed applicant telephones for a decision, the successful applicant should be told he has the job subject to references and should give notice as you will be telephoning his employer for references on Friday. Full and complete details of previous employers should be confirmed with him then, on the telephone, and he should be told the offer will be confirmed in writing with full joining instructions (see example on page 94). If he has been self-employed, or living abroad, or unemployed, you must have the names, addresses, and telephone numbers of two responsible people who will be able to confirm his career history. There must be no blanks but exact dates of starting and leaving each job or other activity.

This procedure, which gives ample opportunity to assess the applicant from two interviewers' viewpoints, as well as from his previous employers' points of view, also helps to eliminate the problem of the 'drop out' who changes his mind at the last moment or who fails to turn up on the joining date.

You have made him:

1. Telephone or call for an interview.
2. Complete an application form in detail.
3. Attend the interview
4. Telephone back to see if he is short-listed.
5. Attend a second interview.
6. Telephone back for a decision.
7. Give notice so that you can take up references.

If he does all these things, he almost certainly wants the job and will not let you down.

If you offer the job by letter, or after only one interview, you may be offering the job to someone who would not be keen enough to fight for it, but has nothing to lose by going through the motions of accepting it while he attends other interviews, hoping to find something he likes better. If he does, he turns the job down or starts with you and drops out during or immediately after induction training.

The ideal timetable would be:

Tuesday   Divisional manager advertises.
Wednesday   9 a.m. to 8 p.m. First interview by divisional manager.
Thursday   Second interview by branch manager (with or without divisional manager)
Friday   a.m. Branch manager makes verbal offer subject to references – notice given to employer.
                    p.m. Branch manager takes up verbal references.
Following Monday week... Commence at school.

If you string out the recruitment process over two or more weeks some powerful but impetuous salesmen will be answering other advertisements and you will find they do not turn up at the second interview, or if they do, they have other irons in the fire and either turn you down or accept the job and then change their minds at the last minute if another job they prefer is offered to them.

If there is more than one good applicant, the application form of your second choice should be kept so that if another suitable vacancy occurs he can be contacted and called in again for a short interview to establish that:

(a) He is still as keen as ever to join.
(b) Nothing has happened meanwhile for you to change your mind about him.
(c) That he has no other irons in the fire.
(d) So that you can talk to his previous employers about him.

You may then be able to offer him a job if he gives notice at once and you obtain satisfactory verbal references.

Once the decision has been made and the verbal references obtained, the details on the application form should be transferred to a personal record card for retention by the branch manager. The official section at the foot of the application form should be completed in full and filed in the personnel files.

Do not forget that most candidates succeed in concealing at least some of their weaknesses. Therefore in the majority of instances the candidate, if employed, will prove less, rather than more, successful than anticipated. Hence, if you have any reasonable doubts concerning his probable success, you would do well to turn him down rather than anticipate (wishfully) that his performance will prove better than the evidence suggests.

It is better to advertise again than to recruit the best of a bad bunch.

Conclusion

Never forget that although the whole recruitment process is designed to enable *you* to recruit the man *you* want, the applicant is looking for the job *he* wants.

If you want him you must *make him want the job* you have to offer.

7

Recruitment – administration

If you follow my advice and condense the recruitment process down to the minimum of four days, or even allow yourself an extra week, it is still vitally important to get the successful applicant on board as quickly as possible, otherwise they will still keep an eye on the 'Situations Vacant' columns.

Most salesmen can leave their existing employment virtually immediately for, although they may be technically required to give one month's notice, in practice, no one wants to keep a salesman on the payroll once he has resigned.

The ideal timescale is to make the job offer on a Friday and commence training on the following Monday week.

Obviously, this procedure will not apply when recruiting highly qualified, highly salaried sales staff, but normally it will.

Because the time schedule is very tight, the administration of a new recruit's entry into the company must be efficient. Not only must it be efficient to be effective, it must be efficient to give the new recruit confidence in the professionalism of the company he has joined, to reinforce his initial enthusiasm for the job.

I have known excellent, enthusiastic recruits travel from one end of the country to the other on a Sunday afternoon only to find that the hotel they had been told was expecting them was not. Sometimes the hotel was expecting them but the room was dirty or there was no evening meal available.

By the Monday morning, instead of arriving full of enthusiasm to commence their induction training course, they arrive sullen and complaining, wishing they had not accepted the job if this was the kind of treatment they were going to receive.

I have run induction training courses in London, Brighton, Camberley, and Croydon. In none of those areas was it easy to find good, cheap accommodation when you needed it at short notice.

I personally shopped around for the best value, clean, comfortable accommodation available and then I booked rooms for my anticipated recruitment programme for a year ahead. The hoteliers and landladies valued this type of booking and gave the salesmen who stayed there special attention. They knew that if any of my salesmen complained to me that they were not getting good service, I would want to know why, and could well take my custom elsewhere.

Most sales training courses require evening reading, so did ours. Some salesmen complained that the lighting in the bedrooms was too poor to allow them to read without eye-strain. The hotels changed all the light bulbs.

On another occasion, our salesmen complained they could not get breakfast in time to leave the hotel at 8 a.m., which they had to do if they were to arrive by 8.30 for the start of each day's training. The hotel changed its breakfast time from 7.30 to 7.15.

What am I saying?

I am saying that if you want to sustain and build on the initial enthusiasm you have generated during the interview process, you not only have to have an efficient administration machine, you have to be seen to have an efficient administration machine; one that is not designed to constrain the salesman but one that is designed to support him.

Obviously, arranging hotel accommodation is not the only part of the administration process when a new salesman is appointed. These are the minimum procedures which I have found necessary to adopt to ensure the successful appointment of a new salesman.

1. Telephone references to be obtained from present or most recent employer or referees.
2. Letter of appointment and company conditions of service to be sent to the successful applicant on the same day that the verbal offer is made subject to satisfactory references, detailing:
   (a) Starting date.
   (b) Reporting procedure.
   (c) Travelling arrangements, accommodation, and expenses during training.
   (d) Salary, commission, quota, minimum standards of performance.
   (e) Documentation.
3. References to be applied for in writing with follow-up system to ensure they are received.
4. Car available if applicable.
5. Accommodation available if applicable.
6. Sales training room prepared for the correct number of recruits.
7. Catering facilities available.
8. Speakers available.

I suppose the administration of the recruitment process starts with the placing of the advertisement.

You have already decided what you want to say and who you want to say it to, so you must either hand over the responsibility of placing the advertisements to an advertising agency or place them yourself.

There is a third method, which is to use one of the recruitment consultancies. Sometimes they generate a pool of applicants by advertising their placement service and then they operate much like a computer dating service, matching the applicant to the prospective employer.

I believe in some fields they provide a valuable service, particularly when the employer is looking for a ready-made representative with established connections, but I have never found myself attracted to the partners they have selected for me.

Another type of 'consultant' or recruitment agency takes larger full display advertisements in the national press which command a great deal of attention and therefore readership. They then sell sections of it to individual advertisers at a profit.

This means that a company that could not afford to take a large full display advertisement in a national daily or a Sunday paper, can enjoy the advantages without the expense.

There is an additional advantage gained by using this medium in that the applicant feels assured of confidentiality if he applies to a consultant, whereas he may be nervous about applying for a job advertised by a competitor or, worse still, an unknown company giving a box number. After all, it may be his employer advertising for a replacement for him!

I must confess that, although I have used this type of recruitment advertisement, on balance I have found it better to place advertisements through my own advertising agent or, if I am advertising at short notice, in many papers at the same time with different telephone numbers and venues, in the classified or semi-display columns, I prefer to place them myself using my local managers.

If they get the advertisement wrong, they have only themselves to blame.

The safest way to ensure the right advertisement appears is to send or deliver to the paper the *actual* advertisement exactly as you want it to appear.

Maybe the first time you place it the paper will set it and, if you like the way it looks, you can photocopy a 'pull' of the advertisement and, with the help of a little Tipp-Ex, change the date and use it on future occasions.

It might look something like this:

Are you looking for a SALES CAREER?

You may find it with OURCO LTD. We have a product with infinite applications in commerce, industry, and the professions. We believe in training our staff to sell professionally, that is effectively and ethically. We believe in a salaried sales force with generous commission to provide the luxuries in life. We believe in internal promotion. If you are under 40, have a car, and consider yourself a quick thinker, call at 65 Bolton Street, Birmingham, tomorrow, Tuesday, between 12 noon and 7 p.m. to see Mr Jones, or telephone 021-123 4567.

OURCO LTD, 19 HARRISON STREET, London W1 Telephone 0181-123 4567

Obviously the timing of the advertisement must take into account the ideal starting date and, if several recruits are needed, the recruitment process must be co-ordinated so that all the successful applicants can receive induction training at the same time.

For the interviews to be conducted effectively, careful thought must be given to the facilities. Obviously, it is ideal if the interviews can be conducted in impressive company premises, but if this is not possible, and it certainly has not been possible for me on every occasion, hire a *good* hotel room, three star at least, preferably four star. Clothes make the man they say, and they are right.

Make sure you have an ample supply of literature and, better still, if you are selling a product or commodity, have samples, point of sale material, photographs of the factory; in fact, all the support material you can reasonably bring to the interview to give the applicant a three-dimensional picture of the company.

The next thing you need is an application form. Most companies already have them, a general purpose document that is used for all types of applicant from driver to draughtsman, labourer to laboratory assistant.

Each company I joined had such a document which did not give me the information I needed to identify the A and B qualities that would eliminate unsuitable applicants, and the positive qualities that would encourage me to short list them for a second interview. I therefore designed an application form that would not only give me the basic information I needed to launch me into my first interview investigation, but gave the applicant the impression that he was dealing with a profitable, professional organization. It was four pages, it was in two colours, but it was easy to read, easy to understand, and easy to complete. A copy of this four-page application form is included at the end of this chapter.

The first page, or front cover, was prestigious, but also gave the applicant reassurance about confidentiality.

Page Two established the stability or instability of the family relationship and also provided a good guide to the financial relationship between husband and wife, in addition to confirming the applicant's ability to absorb and retain information on demand.

As we were an exporting company language qualifications were relevant, period of notice from present employer was critical, and hobbies and leisure activities provided a handle on which we could hang our ice-breaking conversation. Part Two of the form is designed to give us the information we require to evaluate the salesman, continuity of employment, his sales ability, measured in terms of commission rather than gross earnings, and his reason for leaving his present employment.

The box in the bottom left corner of each section 'For office use: Ph.' is for the interviewing manager to complete with a tick or a cross indicating that he has or has not obtained a satisfactory reference from that employer over the telephone.

I would not process an application unless the manager had obtained two satisfactory telephone references. As I have already said, previous employers will always try to do 'the right thing' and help the applicant obtain employment, so the telephone application for the reference must be objective. Never forget that you are giving this applicant control over anything between 10 and 20 per cent of your income. When in doubt – do not!

Naturally, some applicants will not be in current employment. This need not present a problem. Part Three of the application form caters for such a contingency.

First and foremost the career history in Part Two must cover every month of every year, so that there are no months unaccounted for, but if the applicant has been self-employed for a period of time in recent years, or has been unemployed during the past three years, then the names of two referees of substance must be given.

References are of the utmost importance. Never forget that the best, most professional, and most effective salesmen are able to make you believe that they are telling you the truth. They can inspire confidence and you will be absolutely certain that you have discovered the best thing since sliced bread.

If the applicant is genuine and honest, then you probably have, but if he is a con man, the reference should find him out either when you telephone them or, if not then, when you write for written confirmation. The important thing is to follow them up. You cannot ethically telephone a current employer before you have made a job offer and it has been accepted, but you can telephone previous employers and character referees before the offer is made. Where the applicant is employed, the job offer will obviously be subject to satisfactory references being obtained.

Sometimes, people with something to hide will claim they have been in Canada, South Africa, Australia, or the Isle of Wight. Do not let it deter you from applying for references. Fax works wonders, replies come back within minutes, but even a written reference to an overseas employer will normally receive more prompt attention than it would from a firm down the road.

Remember, the object of taking up references is to (a) get positive confirmation that the applicant is honest and hardworking and that he has told you the truth, and (b) that if he was a salesman before he is an above average salesman. If he has not been in the top 50 per cent of his previous employer's sales force, forget him.

No matter what the mitigating circumstances were, forget him.

If you have to rely on written references only, because they could not give you a verbal reference, it is even more important to have a foolproof brought-forward system to ensure that a follow-up letter is sent if a reply is not received in seven days. A follow-up telephone call is even better. Then there must be another brought-forward for a few days hence, otherwise you will sometimes find yourself training a person you should not have recruited.

Having made a verbal offer of employment, having taken up verbal references and put into motion the written confirmation letters, it is necessary to send or give the successful applicant a written letter of employment, which must not only include details of remuneration and terms of employment but also a job specification. It is otherwise impossible to dismiss someone for unsatisfactory performance because if they have not been told what satisfactory performance is you cannot say that performance is unsatisfactory.

Whereas I can see the justice of it, I personally feel that this legislation with all its procedures of verbal warnings, written warnings, and appeal procedures has not encouraged inexperienced people to enter the world of selling. On the contrary, they have to be told 'If you don't generate . . . worth of business in . . . weeks, your employment will be terminated'. Even if they have the guts to accept the challenge, they know there is a sword of Damocles hanging over their head from day one. As each day, each week goes by, the thread suspending that sword becomes visibly frayed, and the beads of perspiration appear on the upper lip. This is no way to give a new recruit the confidence he needs to generate confidence in others. A relaxed and confident salesman generates confidence in others.

Fortunately, the draconian legislation of the 1970s has now been relaxed somewhat, but I still remember as if it were yesterday, being taken to the Industrial Tribunal accused of unfairly dismissing a salesman.

It cost us a fortune with counsel briefed and representing us for two days.

I am normally a well organized, cautious, and competent manager, but on this occasion I acted precipitously, and this is how it happened.

I was sitting in my office one afternoon, engrossed in my normal sales management activities, when the telephone rang. I answered it and the familiar voice of my PA said 'We have an irate customer on the telephone'. 'Put him through,' I said. I heard her hang up.

'Good afternoon,' I said, 'Can I help you?'

'No, I don't think you can help me,' responded the caller, 'But maybe I can help you. We have just been visited by your Mr Sharp. He was obviously drunk, so we told him that we did not want to do business with him. His breath smelt of beer, his speech was slurred, it was obvious that he had been drinking, and when he got back into his car and drove away he had two wheels on the road and two wheels on the pavement.'

I put out a call for Mr Sharp. He did not respond that day, but the following day he came in to see me. I told him of the conversation I had had with our potential customer and asked him for his explanation.

He said that he had been having trouble with his car, which had been stalling and misfiring due to fuel starvation. It had broken down that day and he had disconnected the fuel pipe from the carburettor and had sucked the petrol through from the tank to make sure there was no obstruction or air-lock. In doing so, he had got a mouth full of petrol.

Fortunately, he had broken down outside the Conservative Club where he was a member, so he went in and drank one half pint of beer to take the taste of petrol out of his mouth. Unfortunately, this was not completely successful because he had false teeth and some of the petrol had found its way under his dentures. So he took them out. By now, he was running late for his next appointment so he arrived, no doubt smelling of petrol and beer, with his speech impaired by the lack of dentures.

Obviously, I knew that I could not prove that his story was untrue and yet I knew that I could not, under any circumstances, tolerate a representative of the company giving a potential customer the impression that he was drunk.

What could I do?

I decided that as I could not disprove his story, I must accept that he had consumed only one half pint of beer.

On the other hand, I had to accept that a potential customer was given the impression that he was drunk. Putting those two responses together the conclusion was simple. I told Mr Sharp that when he has only one half pint of beer (based on his own story) potential customers think he is drunk (potential customer's telephone call). Therefore, if he ever drinks even one half pint of beer and then goes on working, I will have no alternative but to dismiss him.

I confirmed this to him in writing.

Some months went by and then one afternoon about 3 o'clock I received a telephone call from an irate potential customer. Our Mr Sharp had telephoned them and had intimidated the receptionist and his personal secretary. Sharp was obviously drunk and the girls were very upset by the abuse that they had received over the telephone.

I naturally apologized and said I would investigate the matter.

I spoke to the sales office staff whose job it was to accept telephone calls from the salesmen as well as to pass enquiries to them.

They confirmed my worst fears. He telephoned in regularly each day, morning and afternoon, as all members of the sales force were required to do, and they all agreed that when he telephoned in after lunch each day, he sounded different, he sounded drunk.

What could I do?

I wrote to him expressing my disappointment that, in spite of my previous warning, it was quite obvious that he was continuing to drink at lunch time and, as a result, was giving the impression to both our office staff and to potential customers that he was drunk. He gave me no alternative but to terminate his employment.

As I have said, he claimed unfair dismissal and the case went to tribunal.

He agreed that he probably had sounded different, possibly aggressive on the telephone that afternoon because he had injured his neck muscles lifting company property into the boot of his car and had been prescribed muscle relaxant tablets by his doctor. Although they were partially effective, he was in great pain but continued to work rather than take sick leave.

The tribunal found in his favour, although they obviously knew he had been drinking as did everyone else. They found in his favour because I did not give him an opportunity to put his side of the case before I dismissed him.

Before this employee protection was introduced I set no standards of performance that had to be achieved for security of employment. I held no sword of Damocles over their heads. On the contrary, I gave every new recruit the confidence, the belief, that he was going to succeed right up to the moment of dismissal. Even at the eleventh hour a marginal recruit would go out selling *believing* that he was going to succeed, projecting confidence and, as a result, many succeeded. On the other hand, many did not.

I did not say 'You have not met minimum targets and therefore I am dismissing you'. I reviewed his progress from day one to date. Obviously, I was going to dismiss him, progress was minimal. I compared his progress with the progress we knew from years of experience was expected from anyone who was suited to our type of selling, on course for a successful career. Naturally, during those unsuccessful, unrewarding weeks, the unsuccessful recruit had been earning very little, far less than he needed to sustain even a modest standard of living and, therefore, if he was not suited to our type of selling the longer he continued the worse off he would be financially. Did it not make good sense, therefore, for him to change direction to find a career more suited to 'his talents'?

Although he had to 'bite the bullet' he would usually agree with me and we would normally part good friends. This, to me, was better than having to give thirty-day warning letters, which not only comply with industrial relations legislation, but stimulate the unfortunate recipient to read the 'Situations Vacant' advertisements more avidly than ever.

There is another reason why I dislike job specifications which detail minimum standards of performance.

They become maximum standards of performance. Obviously, an employer is not going to set a standard at which the salesman is unprofitable but, on the other hand, he cannot set a minimum standard that is unattainable by none but the high fliers. You therefore finish up with a mediocre standard which, if exceeded, makes a salesman feel he has achieved quota and therefore deserves a pat on the back.

I like to set targets, not quotas, and although this chapter is on administration, not motivation, I felt I should record not only what the appointment letter and job specification should include, but my personal feelings on the subject.

Obviously, I had fairly strong feelings about industrial legislation, but what do you think makes a typical salesman's pulse rate increase?

No, I am not talking about that or even salary, or commission, or bonuses, I am talking about cars.

If your advertisement says 'Company car provided' and you give him a van, you probably won't see him again.

If you tell him he is getting a new car and you give him one with 10,000 miles on the clock, you have lost a disciple. If you give him a car with a boot full of pine needles and faulty brakes, you and your company have lost their credibility.

I am not now talking about cars as a motivational tool. I am talking about efficient administration of the fleet. At the final interview, you must know what car, if any, the successful applicant will be given and when it will be available. It does not matter if it is a van if the applicant is told it is a van. The important thing is to ensure that the man you recruit is not let down, not disillusioned by being given a car that falls short of his expectations. Do not forget that he has certainly told his wife and kids and possibly his next-door neighbour that next Friday he is taking delivery of a – well, whatever you told him he would be driving home.

Let us assume that he has managed to escape the many pitfalls in the recruitment process and we now actually have a number of recruits technically on board, regularly appointed, references checked, comfortable in their hotel rooms, confident their cars are clean and serviced just waiting for collection, champing at the bit and ready for their induction training course.

It is from this moment on that the induction training programme can make or break the new recruit.

YOUR CO LTD

**APPLICATION FOR
POSITION AS SALES
REPRESENTATIVE**

Forename ....

Surname ....

**All information given will be considered as strictly confidential and no contact will be made
with present or previous employers without the applicant's consent.**

PART ONE

Forename ....

Surname ....

Address ....

Telephone no. (Home) ....(Office) ....

Date of birth ....Age...................................

Marital status ....Ages of children ....

Wife/husband's occupation ....

Other sources of income ....

Do you own, rent or share your home? ....

If appointed would you provide your own car? ....

School ....

Examinations passed ....

....

....

Tertiary education and qualifications gained ....

Languages spoken fluently ....

Serious illnesses or road accidents ....

....

What notice does your present employer require? ....

Hobbies and leisure activities ....

PART TWO

Career details including Military Service
(Enter present employment first)

From...............

to ....

For office use:
Ph:

Employer ....

Tel no ....

Address ....

....

Head office address ....

Name of manager/supervisor for references ....

Position held and duties...

....

Earnings over past 3 months: salary £............. commission £.........

Why do you wish to leave your present employer? ....

....

....

**PART
TWO
cont.**

From..............
to ....

Employer ....
Tel no ....
Address ....
....
Head office address ....
Name of manager/supervisor for references ....
Position held and duties...
....

*For office
use:
Ph:*

Earnings over past 3 months: salary £............. commission £.........
Why do you wish to leave your present employer? ....
....
....

From..............
to ....

Employer ....
Tel no ....
Address ....
....
Head office address ....
Name of manager/supervisor for references ....
Position held and duties...
....

*For office
use:
Ph:*

Salary: on joining £.............p.a. on leaving £.............p.a.
Final 3 months earnings: salary £............. commission £.........
Why did you change your employment? ....
....
....

From..............
to ....

Employer ....
Tel no ....
Address ....
....
Head office address ....
Name of manager/supervisor for references ....
Position held and duties...
....

*For office
use:
Ph:*

Salary: on joining £.............p.a. on leaving £.............p.a.
Final 3 months earnings: salary £............. commission £.........
Why did you change your employment? ....
....
....

**PART
TWO
cont.**

From............... Employer ....

to .... Tel no ....

Address ....

....

Head office address ....

Name of manager/supervisor for references ....

Position held and duties...

....

| For office use: Ph: |

Earnings over past 3 months: salary £............. commission £.........

Why do you wish to leave your present employer? ....

....

....

**PART
THREE**

If you have not been continuously employed or have been self-employed during the past 3 years, please give the names, addresses and telephone numbers of two persons of substance to whom we may apply for references.

Name ....

Status ....

Firm ....Tel. no. ....

Address ....

....

| For office use: Ph: |

Name ....

Status ....

Firm ....Tel. no. ....

Address ....

....

| For office use: Ph: |

**For Office
use only**

1st	Date and time 2nd	2nd	Date Com.

Referred to ....Branch

Car needed? Yes/No	Hotel Yes/No

Licence no. ....

Signed..............................Manager

Sample Letter of Appointment

COMPANY LETTERHEAD

Dear

I take pleasure in confirming your appointment as Sales Representative, subject to satisfactory references, dating from Monday . . ., when you should report to our reception area at the above address by 9 a.m., to commence one week's induction training.

During this week we shall be responsible for your 2nd class return rail fare to and from your home, also your hotel bill for bed and breakfast. We will also make an allowance of £15.00 per day so that you may purchase an evening meal on each of the five nights that you will be away from home. You should not charge the evening meal to your hotel account because you will claim it on arrival at the course. The initial Training School should finish on Friday at midday.

Accommodation has been booked for you at the . . . for the nights of Sunday . . .

As you will commence in the field on Monday . . . having completed your induction training, your quota for the month of ... will be .... In subsequent months it will be as detailed in the Schedule of Remuneration for Salesmen/women. In the unlikely event of your not securing this quota, the deficit will be carried forward from month to month and monthly thereafter.

This quota is used for the purpose of computing your commission and does not reflect the level of business which the Company considers an experienced member of the Sales Force should attain.

After you have completed your training you will be expected to average not less than . . . sales per month, at least . . . of which must have been generated by your own direct approach or promotional work and not originated from enquiries issued to you by the Company. Where enquiries are issued to you, you will be expected to obtain one acceptable sale from not more than ... enquiries issued. Your continued employment as a Sales Representative is conditional upon these minimum standards being maintained. Under the Employment Protection Act 1975 we are required to notify all employees of our standard Disciplinary and Dismissal Procedure. A copy of this Procedure is held by your Branch Manager and is available for you to read. I am enclosing (1) a second copy of this letter which I would ask you to please sign and return to me in the enclosed envelope by return of post (2) Schedule of Remuneration for Salesmen/women and (3) the Company's Particulars of Terms of Employment, (4) a Pension Scheme Application Form.

To enable us to finalize your hotel accommodation would you please telephone our Personnel Department giving them the approximate time you will be checking into the hotel on the Sunday.

On commencing will you please bring with you (1) a signed Pension Scheme Application Form (2) your Birth Certificate (3) your current Driving Licence and (4) a P45 from your last employer.

Needless to say I hope you will be extremely happy in your new career and rest assured that everyone here will do their best to ensure that you are.

If you feel there is anything I can do to assist you at any time, please do not hesitate to ask.

Yours sincerely,

National Sales Manager

I confirm I have received:

1 Schedule of Remuneration for Salesmen/women
2 Particulars of Terms of Employment
3 Application Form for Pension Scheme

Signed...................................

Date.......................................

Particulars of Terms of Employment

Name of Employee: ....

Date of commencement of employment: ....
(No employment with a previous employer will count as part of your continuous period of employment).

Job Title: Outside Sales Representative

A   *Remuneration*

1   The rate of your remuneration is set out in the attached schedule.
2   Unless otherwise agreed in writing your remuneration will be paid monthly by cheque or bank transfer on the last day of each calendar month.
     Note: Staff do not qualify for overtime payments; however where exceptional overtime is worked at the Company's request employees may be suitably recompensed at the discretion of the Company.

B   *Hours of work*

1   Your normal hours of work are from 9 a.m. to 5.30 p.m. Mondays to Fridays, inclusive, with a lunch break of one hour.
2   If you have special reasons for wishing to be absent you should obtain prior permission from your immediate superior. the company reserves the right to make a pro rata deduction in respect of the period of your absence. In certain circumstances (e.g. attendance at examinations, family affairs of extreme urgency) the Company normally makes no deduction.

C   *Special terms*

1   It is a term of your employment that you shall not, without the prior consent of the Company duly obtained in writing signed by a Director of the Company, engage in any business activity other than the business of the Company and its subsidiary and associated companies.
2   It is a term of your employment with the Company that at all times you shall be the holder of a current valid British driving licence. Disqualification from holding a current valid licence may render you liable to dismissal.

D   *PAYE tax form*

On arrival you must hand in to the Personnel Office a Tax Form P45, properly completed, from your previous employer in order that the correct PAYE may be deducted.

E   *Holidays*

1   You are entitled to the statutory Public Holidays at full pay in addition to your entitlement to annual holidays.

2   All annual holidays must be taken on days agreed with he Company. Not more than 10 working days holiday may be taken consecutively.

3   The holiday year runs from 1 st January to 31 st December. 4 Your entitlement to annual holidays is as follows:

(a) If your employment commenced on or before 1 st January in any year you will be entitled to 20 working days holiday of which 5 days must, if the Company so decides, be taken on specified days.

(b) If your employment commenced after 1st January in any year you will be entitled to one and a half working days holiday in respect of each completed calendar month between the date of commencement of service and the end of that calendar year.

5   Your annual holidays are with pay at the full rate of your basic salary.

6   Any entitlement to annual holiday not taken by 31 st December in any year cannot be carried forward to any subsequent holiday year unless the Company specifically agrees to this.

7   If your employment is terminated, other than by reason of misconduct, before you have taken all the annual holidays due for the holiday year in question you will be entitled to payment in lieu thereof calculated at your basic rate of salary for one and a half days for each completed calendar month of service in the holiday year in question less the number of days holiday actually taken in that year.

8   If your employment is terminated in any holiday year after you have taken some or all of your annual holiday entitlement for that year the Company has the right to make a deduction from your pay of an amount equal to 1/12th of the total holiday pay received by you multiplied by the number of calendar months (or part thereof) between the date of termination and the end of the calendar year.

F   *Sickness or injury*

1   If you are absent from work owing to sickness or injury you must advise the Company of the reason for such absence as soon as possible.

2   If your absence continues for more than two consecutive working days you must send a self certification certificate to the person to whom you report then and thereafter Medical Certificates at weekly intervals.

3   The maximum period and amount of sick benefit to which you are entitled for absence (calculated by reference to your basic rate of salary) is:

During the first 3 months of service	2 weeks at 1/2 pay
During the next 9 months of service	4 weeks at 1/2 pay
During the next 12 months of service	8 weeks at 1/2 pay
Thereafter	16 weeks at 1/2 pay

4   No deduction will be made for Social Security sickness benefits and employees should claim such Social Security benefits if they are absent for more than three days by reason of sickness or injury.

5   In the case of extended absence the Company may, at its absolute discretion, continue to pay benefit for longer periods; special consideration will be given to employees who have been with the Company for several years.

G   *Pensions and pension scheme*

It is a condition of your employment that you apply to become a member of the Pension Scheme on the commencement of your employment or immediately you become eligible for membership. To be eligible for membership you must be a permanent employee and you must be not younger than 20 nor older than 60 (females) or 65 (males). On any question of eligibility the Company's decision shall be final.

Your rights and obligations under the Pension Scheme are governed by the Rules of the Scheme for the time being in force. A copy of the Rules is available for inspection on request. An application form is enclosed which you must complete and return. As a member of the Outside Staff your Pension Scheme Membership will become effective 9 months after the commencement of your employment if you are then eligible. A contracting-out certificate is in force for this employment.

H   *Rights of notice*

1   You are required to give the Company a minimum period of notice of termination of your employment of 1 month.
Notice should be in writing addressed to the person to whom you report.

2   Where notice of termination of employment is given by the Company the minimum period of notice will be as follows:

Length of service	*Period of notice*
Up to 4 years	1 month
From 4 to 12 years	1 week for each year of continuous employment
Over 12 years	12 weeks

The above periods of notice by the Company shall not apply in cases of gross misconduct or to employees who commit an act of bankruptcy or are convicted of a criminal offence. In such cases the Company reserves the right of immediate dismissal without prior notice.

I   *Grievance procedure*

If you have a grievance relating to your employment you should raise it with your immediate superior, either verbally or in writing. If the matter is not settled at this level by the end of the next working day you may ask for it to be passed to your departmental manager who will receive from your immediate superior a note, agreed with you if possible, on how the matter has been handled thus far.

If the matter has not been resolved within a further period of five working days you may ask for it to be dealt with by a Director of the Company.

J   *Trade union membership*

As between the Company and yourself you have the following rights:

(a) To be a member of such trade union as you may choose.

(b) If you are a member of a trade union to take part in its activities at any appropriate time outside working hours and to seek or accept appointment or election and to hold office as an official thereof.

K   *Retirement*

Unless the Company otherwise agrees in writing:

Male employees will retire on their 65th birthday.
Female employees will retire on their 60th birthday.

L   *Alterations*

Any change in these terms of employment will be notified to you in writing.

8

Induction

Most companies use the expressions 'induction training' and 'ongoing training' to distinguish between the initial training programme and the advanced training given to experienced staff.

This division into two training periods is not, to me, an accurate reflection of what is necessary to produce a successful salesman. In the first place, I would question the expression 'induction training'.

Training, to me, is instruction designed to improve the performance of man or beast in a skill, or ability, that he already possesses. For example, a swimmer who can swim will, with proper training, swim faster. A horse that can gallop will, with the help of a trainer, gallop faster.

You cannot train a person who cannot swim how to swim faster, unless you first *teach* him to swim. Therefore, if we recruit potential salesmen who, at the time of induction, do not know how to sell our product or service, we must first teach them how to sell it, not *train* them.

I go further than this. I believe that the word 'teach' implies that, at the end of the teaching process, the pupil can perform that task that he has been taught. For example, if I were to say 'I have taught my son to swim', you would assume that my son could now swim. There is, however, a difference between teaching and instruction. If I say 'I have instructed my son how to swim' you may think I am a bit of an oddball and may possibly ask 'And was the instruction successful?' If I said 'Yes', you may then say 'So you taught him to swim?' If I say 'No', you then think the instruction has been unsuccessful.

You may think this is pure semantics, an examination of the meaning of words, and it is. But there is a real practical purpose for my examination of the meanings of these three words. Let me stay with swimming for a minute and tell you further how I was instructed by the PT instructor at school and, second, how I taught my son to swim.

I suppose we were lucky in those days to have a school swimming pool. It was not very big and it was freezing cold but, once a week, during the summer term, we had compulsory swimming instead of compulsory PT.

Our PT instructor (you note the word *instructor*) was an ex-army sergeant by the name of Simmonds who, for some obscure reason, was known as Sambo. I have no idea why he was known as Sambo, he was bald and pink with large, white, waxed moustaches.

The swimming pool was conventional, with a shallow end and a deep end, but along one side was a row of davits, not for launching lifeboats but supporting a taut wire, rather like the overhead electricity supply for an electrified railway.

On this taut wire was a ring, through which was threaded a rope, on the end of which was a canvas ring approximately two feet in diameter. This was the device that Sambo used to instruct us in the art of swimming. We lowered ourselves slowly into the shallow end of the pool, turning blue inch by inch like litmus paper lowered into an alkaline solution, and placed the canvas ring over our shoulders and around our chests. We leant forward and Sambo took the strain so that we were suspended like Peter Pan in pantomime with our heads above the surface of the water but our bodies just below.

We were instructed in the breast stroke, and slowly and jerkily we would propel ourselves up the pool until Sambo decided it was time to let out some rope. In theory we were supposed to go on swimming oblivious of the fact that Sambo was no longer holding us up, but, in practice, we sank to the bottom like lead balloons.

I do not want to belittle the instruction Sambo gave us. He was very thorough. Before putting us in the canvas harness he had us hanging on to the rail which ran around the edge of the pool, practising the leg strokes. He had us lying on dry land breast-stroking away like stranded frogs. But the truth of the matter is, he did not teach me to swim.

When it was time for me to teach my own son to swim, I remembered Sambo and the good things about his instructional methods. I bought a rubber ring, blew it up, put it on my son and took him into the pool knowing that he could not sink. We mixed play with instruction but, within a few days, he could 'swim' well with the ring inflated. We had races up and down the pool, we had a good time but I was gradually letting the air out of the ring a little at a time until I knew that it was not supporting him in any way.

At a break in play, I asked him if he had realized that his rubber ring was no longer inflated and that he had been swimming without it. He said 'Of course I knew. I'm not daft, Dad'.

I did not then go on to *train* him how to be an Olympic gold medallist. I would not know how, but it helped me to understand the difference between instruction, teaching, and training, and I hope it has helped you.

The transition from instruction to teaching and, more importantly, from understanding what has to be done and being able to do it is probably *the* key stage in the development of successful salesmen. It is 99 per cent the generation and sustaining of confidence.

Some people say that learning to sell is like riding a bike or learning to swim. Once you have learned how, you never forget it. But, how do you learn to ride a bike?

Why is it that for days you can pedal first in ever decreasing circles to the left and then in ever decreasing circles to the right and then, suddenly, you can ride a bike?

I wish I knew all the answers and I do not, but what I do know is that if you are to run a successful instruction, teaching, and training programme, you must recognize that there are these three stages in the development of salesmen.

Let us look first at:

Instruction

Only you know what your salesmen need to know before they can be taught how to sell your product or service. It is probably a lot. It is not only a lot of information that you consider they should know, but what is more important it is how to get them to absorb it that matters most. Never forget that the effectiveness of teaching and training is not measured by the amount of information imparted but by the amount of information absorbed, understood, and accepted as good advice.

Probably the first thing you have to do is to satisfy your new recruit that you are successful, the company is successful, and if you take him under your wing he will be successful. This basic foundation upon which you can build your instruction, teaching, and training programme must be laid during the recruitment process. Not only must you ensure that he wants to learn how to be a successful salesman, in many cases you will have to give him assurance that there are opportunities for promotion that will encourage him to excel as a salesman and thereby qualify for selection as management material.

I remember one of my branch managers projecting such a harassed, overworked, underpaid image that the salesmen in his branch were totally demotivated. Promotion, to them, was unacceptable. Why should they take on the responsibility that weighed down their manager?

When a new recruit joins the company, he must be eager to learn how he can become successful, first as a salesman and subsequently in management.

Therefore, the first instruction he must receive is that there are career opportunities. This is best achieved either by reporting factually on the growth that the company has achieved in the years gone by or by describing the growth that the company expects to achieve in the years to come.

Normally, the first session in an induction course is 'the company'.

You need to project an image of the company that will reassure the new recruit that he has made the right decision. If you have a successful track record produce visual aids and handouts that illustrate dramatically the company's achievements in recent years.

Everyone knows that there are lies, damned lies, and statistics, but I would take this cliché one step further and say that the manner in which statistics are presented gives the professional liar the greatest opportunity to demonstrate his skill.

Let us assume that the company's turnover has increased by 7 per cent per annum over the past five years. This could be illustrated in a graph covering the past five years with a forecast for the next five years, like this:

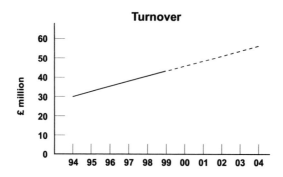

Or like this:

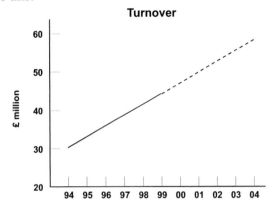

Or, in a 6 per cent per annum inflation environment, like this:

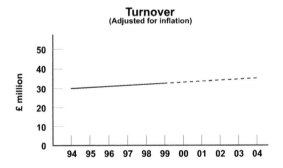

Or, in a 10 per cent inflation environment, like this:

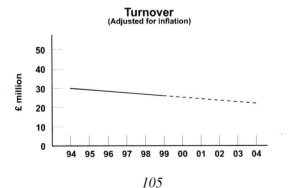

You may even be in a position where you are a newly formed division of a successful group with no track record of your own. In this case you have several options. You can show the group results. You can show the group results plus the sales forecast for your own division, or you can show your own sales forecast on its own, highlighting the projections of growth and proportional opportunities that growth generates. You can even show the growth in the market you are entering.

Not only do you need to present the company's performance or prospects graphically, you need to show the new recruit how this growth has been achieved or how you have planned for growth to be achieved in the future.

There is no doubt that the 'case history' is the best vehicle for this. If you can show that some of the most respected people in the land have decided to buy your product or service, you are well on the way to reassuring your new recruit. Who was it who said 'Bring your witnesses to court'.

I have always produced a 'give-away' pack of information for new recruits which was 'given away' to them at the final interview.

Before the new recruit arrived for his initial instruction course he knew what the company turnover was, he knew how much profit we had made last year and he therefore had a real and truthful picture of the company he was joining.

I have already stressed that this favourable impression must not be destroyed by poor hotel accommodation or, worse still, a disinterested reception by the office staff when he reports on his first day.

Naturally, companies recruiting salesmen vary dramatically in size, in character, and in the numbers they need to recruit.

If a small company recruits one salesman per year, that salesman will probably get the prodigal son treatment.

If a large company recruits twenty to thirty salesmen at a time, they will probably be treated either like a coach-load of package holidaymakers making contact with their courier, or a group of tourists drawn by an invisible magnetism to a Beefeater Guide at the Tower of London, or like an intake of new recruits to the army, or maybe like a Black Maria full of remand prisoners arriving at the Scrubs. It depends upon the attitude of the company's staff.

None of these alternatives is acceptable.

If you have read *The Secrets of Successful Selling* you will know that the most important word in the selling vocabulary is 'confidence'. If your new recruit is to be successful he must not only have confidence in himself, he must generate confidence in the prospects to whom he sells.

Much of this confidence stems from self confidence. If I know that I am more intelligent, more knowledgeable than the person to whom I am selling (and I do), then this confidence will be transmitted in some way to my prospective customer and he will feel confident to take my advice.

Therefore, everything we do in our instruction, teaching, and training programme must be designed not only to instruct, teach, and train, but to build self confidence.

The atmosphere that should be permeated when new salesmen report on day one is that they have arrived to attend a business conference or seminar where all delegates and speakers are of equal intellect. It took me many years to learn that Newton's third law of physics – action and reaction are equal and opposite – applies to human relations in general and sales management in particular. If you respect one of your salesmen, he will respect you. If you despise one of your salesmen, he will despise you. If you work hard for one of your salesmen, he will work hard for you.

Action and re-action are equal and opposite – Newton's third law.

So it necessarily follows that if you want your new salesmen to behave like responsible, knowledgeable, business advisers, you must treat them as such and create an environment in which they identify themselves as such.

I have had to run induction courses in the classroom format due to the large number of salesmen being recruited at one time, and I have run boardroom table courses for ten or less recruits. Sometimes I have trained one new recruit at head office, when it would seem far more cost effective to let his local manager train him at the branch office and thus avoid the cost of transporting him to and from head office, plus the cost of hotel accommodation.

Why did I do it? Why do I still do it?

First, the new recruit has possibly been interviewed in a hotel bedroom and the only impression he has of the company is the two interviewers he has met and the literature they have given him.

Second, there have been many occasions in my experience when the local manager responsible for training the new recruit has also been under pressure to generate business.

If he has to choose between keeping an appointment on Monday morning to close a sale or being in the office to receive the new recruit, he will choose to close the sale.

The new recruit arrives at the local office full of enthusiasm and introduces himself to the branch secretary. She apologizes for the absence of the manager who will be in later and says he has asked her to give him a bundle of technical material to read.

What an anti-climax! What a disappointment! What a demotivating experience!

I decided that even if we were recruiting only one salesman, that salesman should be given the opportunity to visit head office to meet and get to know all the head office personnel with whom he would come into contact over the years, and recognize that he was being treated with the respect that he deserves.

You may think that I am giving undue emphasis to the manner in which new recruits are received on day one, but I am not. Not only is it vital to generate self confidence, it is vital to make the new recruit *want to learn* what he has to learn and what you have to impart. He must feel glad that he has joined the company, he must be keen to be successful, anxious to learn how he can achieve that success.

This brings me to the $64,000 dollar question.

Do you know what information or instruction to give him to ensure that he has all the information he needs to be successful?

If you were to tear up this book or throw away every page but one, then this is the page that you should keep and pin upon the board above your desk, so that you can see it every day.

You must have a proven, successful method of selling the product or service that can be taught to the average salesman who will perform, subject to good management, at a level that is within the company's financial constraints. This was stressed and expanded in Chapter 3 and, if you cannot instruct new recruits in the manner in which they can achieve company targets, then before you go any further you will have to develop and prove a successful method of selling your product or service. You do not have to get the whole sales force using the method, a lot of old stagers who use their own 'special methods' cannot be retrained but most must be retrained. You need to have a teachable method of selling that works for you, and you must teach your managers and trainers how to be successful using your methods for, if the instructors do not have confidence in what they are teaching, what chances have they of instilling confidence in their pupils?

The instruction that new recruits receive will be what they carry with them into the field at the end of their course.

Much of it will be essential, factual information, such as how to document a sale or complete a weekly activity report. They will also be told a great deal about the product or service that they are going to sell.

Sometimes the information will be given to the new recruits by technically qualified people from R & D, production and servicing, because, let us face it, they know a lot more about the product than the sales force does. In my opinion, the sales managers and sales trainers know enough about the product or service to dispense with the need for technical assistance and, by the end of the induction course, no matter who has given the training, the new recruit departs with a portmanteau full of product information even if his head is empty.

There is not time to teach him everything, but one thing he must have is product knowledge. Or must he?

It did not take me long in my sales management career to realize that new salesmen emerging from induction courses were describing features to their prospects, rather than selling benefits. If you do not know the difference read Chapter 19 in *The Secrets of Successful Selling* and you will soon understand the difference.

The tragedy is that nearly every new recruit in nearly every company has to be de-programmed once he gets into the field.

It is not that the induction course has failed to make him enthusiastic, it is not that it has failed to give him a vast amount of vital information, but it has usually failed to instruct him in the manner in which the information should be presented.

If you are a sales manager or sales trainer, forget, for a minute, what you teach your salesmen *after* they have completed their induction course and concentrate on those vital first few days when he is being instructed.

Is he being told of the prospect's needs, the prospect's fears, the prospect's desires, how the prospect earns his living, how he has to compete with competitors?

Or, is he being told only about *your* company's desires and *your* company's products or services.

The unsuccessful new recruit says 'We produce this product which does this, this, and this'. The prospect says 'So what?'

The successful, experienced, re-trained salesman says 'I understand you have this problem?' The prospect says 'What can you do about it?'

So, the *instruction* stage in the development of a successful new recruit should include instruction in the art of *establishing the need* which lays the foundation for selling benefits rather than features.

So, induction is instruction in:

1 The company
- Formation.
- Progress.
- Present status.
- Future plans.
- Current structure.
- If possible, tour of head office. Introduction to key personnel with whom recruit will interface.

2 Contract of employment
Although this information has been given (or should have been given) during the second interview it is necessary to re-state:

- Salary and dates of payment.
- Commissions and dates of payment.

- Bonuses and dates of payment.
- Quotas.
- Special or house accounts.
- Minimum standards of performance.
- Disciplinary and appeal procedures.
- Period of notice.
- Pension rights/BUPA etc.
- Reporting.

3 Administration
- The full documentation of a sale.
- Completion of all daily, weekly, monthly, quarterly documentation.
- Company vehicle reports and servicing.
- Procedures for sick leave, holidays, hotel accommodation if required, statements, requisitions, expense claims.

4 The product range

This is where most induction courses go wrong. They say 'Whereas our competitors have only one size which we can call "medium", we have three sizes – small, medium, and large'.

It is vital that this 'description of feature' approach is abandoned and the benefit approach adopted.

I will leave you to write your own scenario, but there is one golden rule, instruct in the art of selling benefits, not features.

There are other areas where clear instruction is, in my opinion, vital. The first is the approach.

It does not matter whether your first verbal contact with a prospect is with him face to face or over the telephone or through his secretary, it is *vital* that the new salesman is instructed what to say – word perfect, parrot fashion whatever you like to call it, for two reasons.

First, the initial contact will decide if you go any further. You are in or you are out.

If there is a form of words that minimizes the risk of being out and maximizes the chance of being in, does it not make sense to use it?

Second, most salesmen, new or well established, are afraid of failure and rejection.

There are two occasions when the risk is at its highest and they are the same as the risk of an aeroplane crashing. At take-off and at landing. In selling terms, at the approach and the close.

Because they are afraid of failure and rejection, they will minimize as far as they are able the number of occasions when they expose themselves to these risks. They do this by avoiding *cold calls* on new, potential customers and by resisting the temptation to ask for the order because the answer may be 'no' and that would be another rejection.

These fears of rejection and also the fear of being asked questions to which the new recruit has no answer *have to be overcome*, and they can be overcome. You have to remove the unknown, eliminate the need to make decisions, and you can do this by composing a standard approach that works face to face, a standard approach that works on the telephone, and a standard close that can be used on every occasion. Phew!

You must insist that these standard approaches and standard closes are used *word perfect* on *every occasion*, and the instruction in their use is part of the induction programme.

Each new recruit must learn them so well that they can use them as if they were reciting their own name and address. Some new recruits, especially those who consider themselves 'experienced salesmen', will resist this method and decry the whole concept of learning a script. They will say you can tell when a salesman is reciting a script parrot-fashion. What they are really saying is that they are not professional salesmen who, like professional actors, can take the written words and breathe life into them, like Olivier or Redgrave, changing the inflection, the nuance, the meter, even the meaning so that those words, written by the playwright, become their own.

How would it be if these professional actors said 'I cannot use Shakespeare's words' or 'I cannot use Pinter's words' or 'I cannot use Elliott's words' or 'I cannot use Ibsen's words, and make them sound as if they were my own'.

They would never work again as actors.

Of course, the reverse is the truth. Not only do they make these words, written by many different playwrights, sound as if they were their own on the opening night, they make them sound as if they were their own on the one-thousandth performance.

And that is what a professional salesman has to do. If he is not prepared to put on a professional performance time after time, day after day, week after week, month after month, then he will be as effective as an actor who decides he will not repeat Shakespeare's words night after night, but will go on stage and extemporize six nights a week (matinées Wednesday and Saturday).

I hope you will notice that I have referred to the approach and the close as two situations in which a prepared and a rehearsed form of words is essential.

Everything that comes in between should, in my opinion, be tailored to reflect the needs of the prospect. Sometimes, in simplistic situations like selling encyclopaedias, the whole sales presentation can be scripted, but, in my experience, the essential problems to be overcome are:

1. Making cold calls either face to face or by telephone
2. Closing the sale

and these problems can and *must* be overcome by insisting upon a set, proven form of words being used on every occasion.

If the method of approach is by cold calling, then obviously the form of words must take into account the need to speak to receptionists and secretaries before a meeting with the decision maker can be arranged. Detailed ways of dealing with these situations are described in *The Secrets of Successful Selling*.

If the method of approach is by telephone, although the same dragons have to be slain, it is much easier, because a copy of the script can and should be clearly displayed beside the telephone, together with all the answers to the most common objections.

9

Teaching

During the induction programme, the new recruit has been buried under a mountain of information. If he is of average intelligence with an average memory and average recall, he will be able to remember about 10 per cent of it. It is important to realize this. In some companies, new recruits are inducted, swamped with information and sent out into the field to fend for themselves, judged to be *trained*. Not only are they not trained, they have not even been taught.

So, how do you teach? Well, for a start you stop instructing. There is a recognized programme for teaching, which goes like this:

- Prepare him.
- Tell him.
- Show him.
- Let him show you.
- Correct and commend.

- Let him practise.
- Check on performance.

and remember – teach one thing at a time.

Let us pick up the last point first. If you teach one thing at a time it all falls into place.

If you cannot make an appointment to see someone, then that is the end of the story. You will not only fail to see anyone, you will fail to sell.

Obvious, is it not?

So, the first stage in the teaching process is to explain what you are going to teach (prepare him), tell him the actual words you are going to use (tell him), make some calls (face to face or by telephone) and you, the manager, use the officially approved form of words for the approach, and make some appointments (show him).

Then hand over to the new recruit. He has now seen how it can be done either face to face or over the telephone, and it is now up to him to show you that he is equally competent (let him show you). Obviously, he will not be equally competent, but you must resist the temptation to say 'That was awful'. You must judge his performance with pragmatism. By all means correct his mistakes, but commend with exaggerated enthusiasm those elements of his performance which merit congratulation.

Teaching in the field can be counter productive. In *The Secrets of Successful Selling*, page 47, I recount such an experience. Certainly you have to 'prepare him', 'tell him', and 'show him', but if you show him how you can use your considerable skill to convince an almost impossible prospect to do what you want him to do, then most recruits will say 'I can't do that. I think you had better accept my resignation'.

Just imagine, if we go back to swimming, that you were teaching someone to dive. Suppose you were to 'prepare him' by saying 'I am going to show you how to do a reverse treble rotation with pike off the twenty-metre board. Now, to do this, I am going to propel myself as high as I can (tell him) in a corkscrew fashion to achieve the three complete rotations. I shall then be facing away from the board. I shall then adopt the pike position touching my feet and then straighten out so that I can enter the water without making so much as a ripple'.

You show him (applause from admiring onlookers).

'Now, let's see you do it!' (let him show you).

If this was day one for him I do not think he would try. I think he would lose heart. At best, I think he would say, 'Can't I try something simpler?'

Teaching selling is no different. You have to break the selling process down into teachable stages, so that the pupil will not only be able to make progress, but will be able to see that he is making progress. If you are to sustain the enthusiasm of a new recruit you must make it possible for him to feel that he is making progress towards his ultimate goal of professionalism and high earnings.

So start off with the approach. If you respond to enquiries the approach is simple. You pick up the telephone and say 'Good morning Mr Bloggs, my name is Adams of Wantuwant Ltd. Thank you for your enquiry about our services. I shall be in . . . next Monday as it so happens. Will you be in your office at 9.30, if I call to see you then?'

Naturally, a percentage will say 'Well, it was just a general enquiry, can you send me literature?' You say 'Well, as I am going to be close to you on Monday, I will drop it in and go through it with you because it is not that easy to understand the differences in the services we offer just by reading our standard brochure. I look forward to meeting you on Monday. Is 9.30 okay?'

I use an additional earpiece on the telephones used for appointment making, so that the pupil can hear both sides of the telephone conversation when I am making the appointment and, conversely, I can listen in when my pupil is making the appointment. I recommend you to have these additional earpieces fitted if you have not done so already.

Obviously, it is more difficult to make an appointment if you have not had an enquiry.

The need to teach by example is therefore even more important. For a start, you *must* have a script. If it is a telephone script, you can have it in front of you while you are on the telephone and during the induction course, but if it is a face-to-face, cold-call script, it must be learned until it can be recited as easily as your name and address.

You are naturally going to be in the field with your new recruit the following week, so if you are making telephone appointments, it is quite natural and logical for you to make the first few appointments that you will keep together and then 'let him show you'. During that week's instruction, he should book a full week's appointments if that is the way you work.

I know it sounds almost stupid to say that if you do not see anyone you will not sell anyone, but it is a truism that is worth remembering. Whereas I have sometimes had a failure when the salesman was getting face to face with prospects I have never had a success when the salesman was not.

If you do not use the telephone but call directly upon likely prospects, the theory remains the same, but the practice is different. It is not normally possible to call on prospects during the induction course so the *'instruction'* training is role play.

The words are not very different and the manager prepares, tells, and shows as before, but a genuine appointment is not made. The new recruit then shows the instructor (let him show you) and the instructor corrects and commends.

The actual teaching process begins in week two, or whenever the new recruit is allowed out on an unsuspecting world. I have worked both these systems.

If you are a competent sales manager, you will not allow him out on his own assuming that he has been *trained* during his induction course. You will realize that he has received a great deal of instruction, virtually no teaching, and certainly no training.

So you will go out with your new recruit on day one in the field and will prepare him for what is about to happen. You will tell him what you are going to say to the first prospect and you will then show him how to make an appointment face to face or go down fighting in the attempt. *You* must go on until you have made one or two appointments. Do not forget that the new recruit has been told that if he uses this form of words he will obtain so many interviews from so many attempts, and it is therefore vital that you perform at this level.

If you do, and you must, you will give your new recruit the confidence he needs to emulate your example.

It is easy to assess the performance of salesmen making

appointments. If it is a telephone approach, the salesman can use a 'tick sheet' which shows the number of dials, the number of speaks to the DM (decision maker) and the number of appointments. If it is a face-to-face call you can similarly record on a 'call sheet' the number of calls, the number of conversations with the DM, and the number of appointments.

Do you use a tick sheet or a call sheet or do you trust your salesmen to tell the truth?

I hate to say this, but even if you do use a tick sheet or call sheet some of your salesmen will still not tell you the truth.

In Chapter 3 I recalled my experience with Adam, who sent me all those phoney orders from Eden. I am not saying that without close control most salesmen will send in false orders, but I am saying that with close control it will be easier for you to detect any peculiarities in work pattern.

By nature I am a logical person. I believe that if you drop ten tennis balls on to a tennis court from a height of three feet, they will bounce to a height of between two feet and two feet three inches. If one of them does not, then something is wrong.

One call sheet means nothing to me, but if I see ninety-nine, which give me a pattern, and the hundredth does not conform to this pattern, I want to know why. Ninety-nine times out of a hundred it is because the information given on the one hundredth sheet is false.

So that I could judge if the information was false and what the mean performance should be, I always spent some time in the field doing the job myself, establishing a norm for the number of calls per day, the number of interviews per day, and the number of sales per day or per week or per month, dependent on the product or service I was selling.

I remember reviewing an unsatisfactory salesman's performance with his manager when on the face of it the salesman had made a lot of calls but had failed to make any sales. We interviewed him together and he put up a convincing performance, assuring us that it was a tough area, hit by recession. I took his call sheets, got into my car and drove to the area he had been working. I called on every prospect he had recorded and not one of them could remember him calling on them that week.

Other salesmen record a pathetically low call rate. How can I say their call rate is pathetically low? Because I either go out with them and record the number of calls that can be made in an average day's work, or I work on the telephone with them to establish how many calls you can make in an hour or even half an hour, and what the result should be.

Just recently, I brought seven experienced salesmen together and asked them to dial ten times (on seven different telephones) so that we could establish how long it took to make ten dials and what results we should expect. All seven completed their ten dials in under thirty minutes and, collectively, they made nine firm appointments. From that experiment, which I have repeated many times with similar results, we can conclude that in our business you can make ten dials in thirty minutes and that you will make at least one appointment in that time. In a seven-hour day you should therefore make not less than fourteen appointments, but in practice none of those salesmen makes more than seven appointments from a day on the telephone.

In the salesman's contract of employment he is required to make not less than seven new appointments each week, so what lessons can we learn from this experience?

First, it is vital to teach an approach that works over the telephone or face to face, so that the average salesman will make firm appointments with sufficient prospects.

Second, it is vital to monitor performance to check that each experienced member of the sales force is generating enough new prospects to ensure a profitable level of business.

Third, a minimum standard of performance written into a contract of employment will often produce that minimum level of performance.

So, what comes next? Well, if you have made the appointment you now embark on the sales process and most of us agree that that can be encapsulated by the mnemonic AIDA (*a*ttention, *i*dentity, *d*esire, *a*ction). We have also agreed that you must teach one thing at a time. So we have to start by teaching how to command 'attention'. It is the process which establishes communication between salesman and prospects, an empathy, a bond, so that what follows will be a flow of information in both directions from one to the other.

I find this *the* most difficult stage in the sales process to teach. It is easy to pin labels on people and I will resist the temptation, but some new salesmen think that the best way to get attention is to dive straight in with the benefits their product or service can offer, whereas others think that they must start by talking about their company's track record to establish credibility. I am not for one moment implying that credibility and benefits should not be presented, but I am certain that they will not gain attention, establish empathy, and create a bond in the first few moments of a meeting. You have to teach your salesman the basic truth, hard to swallow as it may be, that your prospect is not interested in you, he is interested in *him*. If you want to get him interested in *you*, you must first show that you are interested in him. In business the *u* (you) comes before the *i* (I). Never forget it.

Although it is a cliché, a salesman has to sell himself. What do I mean by that? I mean that a salesman will be more successful if the prospect wants to give him the business than if he does not. This has nothing to do with the prospect's needs or the quality of the product. There are countless examples of people paying more than they need because of customer loyalty. It may be that they get better service, it may be because they trust the salesman and know that if ever they were in trouble he would solve the problem for them.

Let us not try to analyse in detail the reasons for customer loyalty, but simply accept that once we are face to face with a prospect the first thing we have to do is to gain his attention and the best way to do this is to take an interest in *him*.

In my first selling job, the 'attention' part was scripted for me. I was selling encyclopaedias for children, so naturally I was questioning about the children. How old are they? How many children are there in their class at school? These are the u questions. They felt that I (i) was interested in them (u) and indeed I was.

Suppose instead of asking about their children, about the number of children in each class, the amount of individual attention that *their* children received at school, and the ways in which they could help their children at home, I had talked about the company. Suppose I had told them how many years had been spent compiling the encyclopaedia, how many people had been involved, how much it had cost. Do you think I would have commanded the same attention? Of course not.

So you, as the sales manager, must devise a form of words that your salesman will use to generate attention, communication, a bond that will make the prospect want to hear what the salesman has to say. Maybe the answer is to give the salesman a questionnaire, which he *must* complete before the sales presentation can commence. In document form it may seem cold and inquisitorial, but presented as an ice-breaker it could prove to be the vehicle which enables the interview to move forward from a cold start to a friendly relationship.

The questionnaire could read:

1	Manufacture:	Yes/No.
2	Type of product:	....

In practice, this would be presented by the salesman as 'I had no idea you had a manufacturing capability here, what do you make? Do you have other plants? Where are they? What do they make? How long have you been making them? What competition do you have? etc., etc., etc.'

Take my advice. Accept that a new salesman is so full of product knowledge and enthusiasm for the benefits the product can bring that he will forget the vital 'attention' stage of the interview unless you script it in for him.

The same will apply to the 'identity' process of the sales presentation.

In Chapter 8, I stressed the need to lay the foundation for the need. This is vital if your prospect is going to identify with the product or service you are selling.

You cannot sell fillet steak, no matter how tender, to a vegetarian.

Probably the third stage in the sales process, generation of desire, is the most easily recognized as the foundation of the salesman's endeavours, but it must not be forgotten that without the effective generation of attention and identification, the generating of desire would be an uphill process.

Hopefully, during the attention and identification stages of the presentation, a strong foundation for the need has been established and the generation of desire then becomes the most easily taught part of the sales process.

I have always used the 'So what?' and 'Which means that' processes of teaching.

I ask a new recruit why I should buy his product rather than a competitive product.

Nine times out of ten he will give me a feature rather than a benefit.

He will say 'It is bigger!' or 'It is cheaper' or 'It will last longer' or 'It is state of the art technology'.

My response to these 'feature' statements is 'So what?'

If you pursue this line of questioning you will end up with the benefit.

'It is cheaper' – 'So what?'

'You need less money to buy it' – 'So what?'

'You won't have to borrow so much' – 'So what?'

'Your interest charges will be lower' – 'So what?'

'You will make a bigger profit' – 'So what?'

'You will be able to buy that new Jaguar you want!' there is no 'So what?' to that.

The whole process could have been short circuited if the salesman had said 'It is cheaper, which means that . . .'

I found that I had to work very closely with my salesmen in the field, not only to teach and train them but also to identify their weaknesses that needed to be strengthened.

Sometimes they were failing to gain attention, to communicate. Sometimes they were failing to establish the need, sometimes they were failing to sell the benefit. But sometimes they were succeeding in all these areas but failing to close the sale.

In the induction course I gave new recruits one or two standard closes that they could use. When teaching them in the field I found that they seldom used them. Do not ask me why, I do not know, but if I gave them a proven, surefire method of closing a sale, like 'You can see why so many people are using this product can't you? And it would be just as useful to you, would it not? Our next delivery to this area is Tuesday of next week, would that be soon enough for you?' They did not use it, they said. 'Well, what do you think?'

Teaching is getting them to use the basic techniques in which they have been inducted.

Training is another matter altogether.

10

Training

Training is an ongoing process. Athletes and horses have trainers all their lives. The trainer's job is not to teach them how to run or how to gallop, but to improve their performance and ensure that they are in peak condition on race day.

You may think that I am stretching the imagination when I compare a salesman to an athlete or a racehorse. I do not think I am. Each of them has to compete in a highly competitive environment, each is hoping to achieve kudos or financial reward, and usually each is capable of far more than was realized before the training commenced.

When I was a salesman, I received no training. I had to buy books which improved my performance dramatically.

Strange as it may seem, I was never motivated by the money I would earn. I was motivated by the need to become better and better and to excel over the other members of my sales team – by kudos, I suppose.

I am certain, in my own mind, that top sportsmen and women like

Tiger Woods, Martina Hingis, Jonatha Edwards or Steve Backley give of their best either to set a new world record or to beat their rivals. They earn a lot of kudos which they need to recharge their egos and last, and probably least, they put a lot of money in the bank.

Race-horses never think of the prize money.

Salesmen are, in the main, more like athletes than racehorses .

They do think of the prize money, because most of them live far beyond their means. If they earn £3,000 in one month they will assume that they will earn £36,000 per annum and set their standard of living accordingly, but they are highly motivated by the challenge to break new records, the opportunity to be respected as a new 'champion', and by the need to establish themselves as the 'best in the branch', the 'best in the sales force', 'the best in the world'.

I know that in sales management you cannot make a silk purse out of a sow's ear.

I know that for a salesman to be a Tiger Woods or a Martina Hingis he has to have a talent equivalent to that possessed by Tiger Woods or Martina Hingis.

Let us stay with that for a minute.

The whole induction, teaching, training process is designed to produce salesmen who are above average.

For a salesman to be above average he needs talent. During the induction and teaching processes there is ample opportunity to gauge whether a new recruit has talent. If he has not he should not be retained, for he would be wasting the time of the 'trainers'.

Can you imagine sending a horse with no 'talent' to a trainer?

If I may digress for a minute. During my days as a farmer's pupil to Bill Manning, I was given a young horse to ride at exercise and later to hounds. He was a big bay horse called Huntsman. I was not a good horseman, but this horse was, for me, perfect. He had the softest mouth you could imagine. Horsey people would say 'Like a piece of silk'. That meant that he would obey the slightest command he felt on the bit in his mouth through the reins I held in my hands.

But he was fast. He was powerful. He had the ability to accelerate and gallop faster than any other horse I had ridden in my very limited experience of the huntin', shootin', and fishin' fraternity.

I rode him to hounds on several occasions with a slack rein, and he cantered along at what was for most a fast gallop. Inevitably he was sold to someone who not only wanted to hunt him but also to race him in point-to-point races.

When his first race came around, I could not go, I had to work, but I asked Bill Manning to put £10 on him for me because I knew he would win.

I spent the day on the tractor and come nightfall I returned to the farmhouse for supper and to collect my winnings.

'Well, how did Huntsman go?' I asked.

'Fine, fine,' said Bill Manning.

'Well, how much did I win?' I asked.

'Nothing, I'm afraid,' said Bill, 'They told me before the race that they did not want to do more than show him the fences in this first outing, so his jockey rode him on a slack rein at the back of the field and he cantered past them all and won. But nobody backed him!'

Huntsman had talent.

I do not suppose you know what talent is any more than I do. I think it is an inbuilt ability to perform well above the norm in a certain art, craft, or discipline, but if you recognize someone with talent then that is the person that will respond most to training.

An obvious example is the talented musician. I do not know what percentage of the population are taught or encouraged to play a musical instrument, but I reckon it is pretty high. My brother and I were both given piano lessons. That is what I now call 'instruction'. We were *taught* how to read music so if you put the two together you will see that we could read the notes but our fingers did not always obey.

Naturally, we were given hours and hours of instruction on particular pieces and practised them for even longer, but the end result was never pleasing to the ear.

Why not? Because we had no musical talent and could therefore never respond to training.

Compare this with *Masterclass*, a marvellous television programme, when truly talented young musicians were privileged to receive training from the likes of Goossens, Menuhin, or Duprés. For these talented youngsters to become masters in their own right they have to be trained in the art of interpretation of the composer's music through their chosen instrument. And what is a salesman's chosen instrument?

It is his voice and his vocabulary.

How many salesmen receive voice training? Hardly any, and yet it is the salesman's voice that is the medium of communication between him and his prospective customer.

I was extremely fortunate in that when I was in Australia driving a hire car for a living, a radio announcer passenger of mine suggested I should try to get a job as a radio announcer. I gave several auditions and the chief announcer of 3KZ Melbourne suggested that I should get some training. This was long before I became a salesman, but the voice training I received for one hour a day, five days a week for nine months, has been one of the major reasons for my success as a salesman.

It has nothing, or very little, to do with accent or dialect. Obviously, a Scot with a broad Glaswegian accent will find it difficult to communicate with an East End cockney and vice-versa.

But, assuming that the talented salesman speaks clearly with or without a regional accent, then speech training can be extremely valuable.

There are five different areas where speech training can be helpful. They are:

- Tone.
- Pitch.
- Timing.
- Content and grammar.
- Pertinence.

Tone is not always as 'trainable' as one would like. Some of us are born with deep, impressive voices like Ed Morrow or Winston Churchill. Some of us are born with thin, reedy voices. Now, do not ask me why, but most people are more inclined to respect the advice given by a man with a rich, deep brown voice, than that given by a man with a highpitched voice. The same applies to women. The low, authoritative tones of a Barbara Stanwyck or a Lauren Bacall are taken more seriously than the high-pitched tones of Ami McDonald or Sandra Dickinson. There is absolutely no logical reason for this for, as far as I know, Ami McDonald and Sandra Dickinson may be far better informed and more intelligent than Barbara Stanwyck or Lauren Bacall. Which goes to show how large a part emotions play in the sales process, often pushing logic aside.

So, if it is a fact, and it is, that low voices carry more weight than high voices, training in lowering and enriching the tone of the voice is worthwhile. I believe this can be achieved by drinking large quantities of whisky or gin, but a cheaper and more practical method is to exercise the vocal chords regularly in one of two ways.

The first is to hum up and down the scales. Obviously it helps if you can do it in private because otherwise friends and neighbours start whispering about you behind your back. A good place is in the car. You can hum away to your heart's content with all the windows closed and no one will even know you are doing it. If you take this exercise seriously, you will gradually increase the length of each note to improve your breath control and you will increase the volume naturally as your vocal chords will allow. You will be surprised at the difference this form of vocal exercise, if performed daily, will make to the tone and timbre of your voice. If you spend ten or fifteen minutes exercising every day on the way to your first call, you will get all the benefit when you arrive.

Another excellent exercise is to whisper. (It was Chico Marx who said, when caught kissing a chorus girl, 'I was whispering in her mouth!'). Most of us use a fairly standard if not scripted sales presentation. Again, driving to your first appointment, go through the whole presentation, whispering it gradually louder and louder as your larynx relaxes until what you are saying is clearly audible, but a loud whisper. Although driving along in your car is again an ideal setting for this exercise, you must accept that the driver in front of you, watching you in his rear vision mirror, will conclude that you have gone completely round the bend, as will drivers who pull up beside you at the traffic lights.

Pitch must be variable and must go up and down in the right places. Obviously, if we drone on and on with every word at the same pitch what we say will sound very boring. We are now getting into the subtleties of why some people are raconteurs and some are bores.

If you listen to a professional actor on the radio, he sounds quite different from the Albert Bullock, 52, of Tooting, when being congratulated on being the first person to grow a vegetable marrow in a bottle.

Halfway between these two extremes are weather forecasters. They have been given some training and they know that they must vary the pitch to keep it interesting, and they go:

First of all, the forecast for the South East
It will start of sunny in the morning but cloud will develop
in the afternoon

Sometimes they go:

And now the forecast for the weekend which will be sunny for most of you

Gradually, this rhythmic presentation of high down to low and back to high will mesmerize you and you will miss that part of the forecast you particularly wanted to hear.

Variation in pitch must not be used to compose a lullaby; it must be used to ensure that the important key words are heard by the listener. That weather forecast should look like this:

First of all, the forecast for the South East.

It will start off sunny in the morning but cloud will develop in the afternoon.

This accentuation has nothing to do with volume but everything to do with pitch. You can change the meaning of phrases completely just by changing the pitch of each word in the phrase. To illustrate this point, in the following sentence the word in italics is spoken at a higher pitch than the other words in the sentence – not louder.

It was *John* who walked to London (not Bill).

It was John who *walked* to London (he did not get the train).

It was John who walked to *London* (not Birmingham).

So the whole meaning of a sentence can be changed by changing the pitch or the inflection that the salesman puts on the individual word.

Obviously, training a salesman to use pitch or inflection does not want to revolve around parlour games, 'How many different meanings can you get out of this sentence?' but should be designed to help a salesman to communicate and ensure that the important benefits are not only described, but heard, understood, and taken on board.

Timing is of equal importance.

Let us get rid of the obvious problems first. If you speak too quickly, there is every possibility and probably a certainty that a lot of what you say will not be understood and absorbed. If you speak too slowly, you will lose your prospect's attention and overrun the time he has allotted you.

So you have to speak slowly enough to be heard clearly, but fast enough to retain interest.

But the most important of all, you must vary the pace and use the pause. This does not mean that you speed up and slow down just for the sake of it; it means you can add drama and importance to words by slowing down certain phrases. Let us look at an example:

'I understand you have four hundred employees. Is that right, Mr Hyram?'

'I understand you have four . . . hundred . . . employees.... Is that *right*, Mr Hyram?'

Here we have used a change of timing and pitch to dramatize and to inject importance into what could have been a mundane, commonplace statement of fact. Obviously, it would be self defeating to overplay this type of situation, but if emphasis is needed there is no better tool than timing coupled with pitch.

They say 'It ain't what you do, it's the way that you do it', which could be paraphrased to 'It ain't what you say, it's the way that you say it', but this is not completely true.

Certainly the way that you say it is important, but what you say is just as important.

First, the vocabulary. The range of words at the command of the salesman are like the notes on the piano or the colours on the palette. The fewer there are the more limited is the musician or the painter.

Most of us have a comprehensive vocabulary of nouns. We know that a bedroom is a bedroom, a car is a car, and an oven is an oven. But adjectives seem to drop through our memory's sieve.

So many salesmen will say 'It's a nice bedroom, isn't it?' or 'It's a nice car, isn't it?' or 'It's a nice oven, isn't it?'

Even without Roget's Thesaurus (which every salesman should buy from his local bookshop) the talented salesman will find better adjectives, or adjectival phrases, than 'nice' to 'desirable features'.

'This is a bedroom to relax in, isn't it?' which means that . . . 'This is a quality car' which means that . . . or 'This is a chef's oven' which means that....

Not only has the talented, professional salesman a need for a full vocabulary, a full palette of colours, he must have the ability to use that palette of colours to paint verbal pictures .

Now you may think that pictures are flat, two dimensional distortions of the true world, but they are not. If you look at a portrait of a man, you will stand and stare and sum up his character from the look in his eye, the flare in his nostril, the curl in his lip, the tilt in his shoulders, the quality of his clothes, the impression that the artist has created by brush strokes of colour on canvas.

So does the professional salesman present his case. There are, however, many talented salesmen who have not yet reached their true potential because they have a very limited command of the English language and no understanding at all of how the language can be used to stimulate the emotions.

It is difficult in 'cold blood' to illustrate the way in which a choice of words can make or break a sale, but if you are training a competent salesman you have to listen carefully to the words he uses to generate desire to buy, and see if they can be improved.

Let us imagine that an encyclopaedia salesman has reached the crucial stage in his presentation when he has to get agreement that the prospect recognizes the need and agrees that it would benefit the family to own an encyclopaedia.

He says 'Well, from what I have shown you so far, can you see that no matter what subject interests you there is a wealth of information available, virtually the answer to every question you or the children may ask. A true asset in the home, don't you agree?'

He closes an acceptable level of sales.

His closing rate might well improve if he said, 'Naturally you want to give your John and Mary all the help you can to get them started on the careers they want, yes?

'I don't have to tell you that whether they want to join the bank, go to university, or take up nursing, the first hurdle they have to jump is GCSEs, true?

'I am sure you know that when the examiners start marking examination papers they decide the level at which they will award an 'A' pass. If you are one mark above, you get it. If you are one mark below, you don't.

'Now, if by having an encyclopaedia in the home John and Mary gained that *one* extra mark that gave them a pass instead of a fail, then I am sure you will agree that the small investment today would be amply recovered. Don't you agree?'

The use of words is naturally reflecting the basic structure of the selling process. Experienced salesmen can understand the reasons for structure so, during the 'training' stage of a salesman's development, I have found it tremendously helpful to discuss, in detail, the theoretical, as well as the practical aspects of selling.

Every sales manager knows that you have to sell benefits. They can be identified as the product of the feature.

But, what comes before that?

You have to establish the need and lay the foundation. This simple procedure is detailed in *The Secrets of Successful Selling*, page 182. You cannot get anyone to buy something they do not want. It is difficult to get anyone to buy something they do not need, so to give yourself the maximum sales opportunities you have to start by identifying the basic reason (the foundation) for the need.

I have never sold hot-air hand driers, but if I were to, I would not extol their virtues in terms of how many cubic feet of hot air they pump out per minute, unless I was competing with a less efficient dryer, and even then I would start off by establishing the need for a hot-air hand drier.

What are we really selling? What is this foundation for the need? It must be to reduce overheads without reducing the quality of the service. So, how do we use words to help us?

Let us lay a foundation.

'Obviously, Mr Prospect, there is a good margin on food and drink. I suppose the major problem is the cost of the overheads. Is that right? So you would welcome anything that would reduce your overheads. Yes?'

It is important to note that at this stage no mention has been made of hand driers or paper towels or roller towels.

We are simply establishing a foundation, a need to reduce overheads for them and we can introduce features (hot-air hand dryers) which will give the benefits that fill the established needs (lower overheads).

Naturally, the salesman selling hand towels will lay a different foundation for his sale.

He will home in to the fact that, if you have a restaurant the number of customers is limited to the number of tables. If you have an hotel, the number of guests is limited to the number of rooms. Yes? So the only way to increase revenue and profit is to increase the price of the meal or the rate for the room. Right?

Now, I am sure you will agree that discerning people will patronize restaurants and hotels where they feel that their patronage is appreciated and valued, where they are made to feel welcome.

Comparatively small things raise the standard on to another plane.

Hot-air dryers in the loo, or lavatory (not toilet), would completely destroy this image, don't you agree? You must have towels, mustn't you?

Training is a never ending process. Athletes have trainers for ever. So should salesmen, even more so. Athletes have a clearly defined objective, 100 metres, 200metres, long jump, or high jump.

Salesmen have a complex and difficult discipline to master. They have to make appointments to see people. They have to gain their attention. They have to establish that a need exists and that the product or service they are selling fills that need. Finally, they have to obtain a signed order, often with a cheque, before they can earn the week's wages.

Our responsibility as sales managers is to ensure that every salesman under our control is trained to a high level of efficiency in each of the areas of responsibility.

11

Controls

If you have a secretary you will know whether or not she (or he) arrives at 9 a.m. and leaves at 5. 30 p.m., because you will be there. You will also know whether or not she can type at 60 w.p.m., by the volume and quality of her work. You will also know, within a week, if she is intelligent, if she thinks on her feet, and maybe other things about her which are outside the scope of this analysis.

If you employ a salesman you will not know if he starts work at 9 a.m. or if he continues to work until 5.30 p.m., or how effective he is in his professed skills without adequate controls and reporting procedures.

It makes me sad to say it but, in my thirty years of sales management experience, I have met many salesmen who were not prepared to do an honest week's work for an honest week's pay.

Sometimes this was because they could exceed the company's minimum standards of performance without working five full days a week.

Sometimes it was because they had other business interests.

Sometimes they had a low 'comfort level' – they could earn what they needed in two days and would rather play golf on the other three days a week than do an honest week's work and earn more than twice as much.

Sometimes they were dishonest, like Adam. Sometimes they were petty thieves falsifying expense claims or 'fiddle sheets' as some people prophetically call them.

Only today I heard of a competent salesman earning in excess of £30,000 p.a. being dismissed for changing a petrol receipt from £5 to £15. Simple controls which compared petrol expenditure with mileage caught him out.

But controls are not always designed to detect misconduct, far from it.

In the main, they are designed to act as aids to management, information providers that enable both manager and salesman to operate as efficiently as possible but, to get it out of the way, let us look firstly at the control of expenses.

This is an important area because not only can expenses become a major component of direct sales cost, they can become an important influence on the morale of the sales force.

Employers can be seen as a 'good touch' or 'miserable sods' even when the 'good touch' pays poorly and the 'miserable sod' pays generously, purely due to the way expenses are controlled.

In Chapter 15, which deals with remuneration, the alternative methods of paying expenses are explored, but whatever method is applied the control system must be designed to ensure that the salesman knows exactly what he can claim and what he cannot and is paid promptly for all legitimate claims. On the other hand, it must ensure that he is not paid money to which he is not entitled.

At Gross Cash Registers and Ansafone I controlled expense claims with the bluntest of instruments. I paid salesmen a flat rate which had to cover all expenses incurred on the territory. If they were required to move off their territory to visit Head Office or attend a branch meeting, they were reimbursed for the extra travelling or hotel expenses incurred, but otherwise they could not claim anything.

My philosophy behind this policy was simple. I wanted each salesman to work his territory to a plan, minimizing travelling time by block canvassing, and if he did this he would make a profit out of his expense allowance. If, on the other hand, he wasted selling time by driving around unnecessarily, not only would he be spending time unproductively, he would be spending his own money filling up the tank with petrol. There was also another consideration.

I had four hundred salesmen, plus one hundred managers. It was bad enough having to check, authorize, and pay one hundred managers' expenses. To do the same for four hundred salesmen was an administrative burden I could not justify.

You could say that I did not pay expenses at all but I did pay an untaxed allowance and supplemented it, if authorized by management, with extraordinary off-territory expenses.

The control documentation was a form completed by the manager, not the salesman, which said:

Please pay to ....the sum of £.............. in respect of .... miles travelling off territory on my authority and the sum of £ .... for overnight accommodation as detailed in the attached receipt.

Signed ....

I do not know of a simpler, more effective way of controlling expenses, but it is obviously an inappropriate method in many situations.

I have been required to spend two or three weeks at head office when I incurred virtually no expenses. I have then spent two or three weeks travelling to Australia and Japan.

Obviously, a fixed expense allowance would be totally inappropriate for me. In between these two extremes we find the norm and it is in this area that the control philosophy, the contract of employment, and control documentation must be unambiguous.

The contract of employment must detail the type of expenditure for which reimbursement can be claimed. It must be explained to the new recruit that no other claim will be entertained. Let me give you an example.

In my present company we provide our sales force with all the stationery items they require and a supply of stationery requisition forms. It covers everything from staples to carbon paper. If a salesman does not order staples on his stationery requisition, but submits a receipt for the purchase of staples from W H Smith with his expense claim and asks for reimbursement, the claim will be disallowed, because he knows supplies of staples are available from the stationery department.

So the expenses claim form must *never* be:

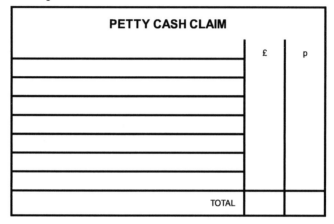

It must itemize each type of expenditure for which a claim is acceptable and build controls to justify the claim. The speedo readings are essential, managers' written approvals for hotel accommodation are also, as are receipts for everything other than telephone-box calls, parking meters, tube and bus fares. Such a form will not only ensure that the honest salesman will receive reimbursement promptly, but will make it difficult for the slightly bent salesman to get away with a minor indiscretion.

You could say that this is a negative subject in sales terms and I would not disagree with you, but the negative aspect is in having to disallow a claim for expenses and this is extremely demotivating; it generates a great deal of resentment. If your contract of employment is right, if your controls are right, you will have no disputes and prompt payment will generate goodwill.

Salesman..................

Territory..................

EXPENSES CLAIM FOR W/E..................

ITEM	MONDAY	TUESDAY	WEDNESDAY	THURSDAY	FRIDAY	SATURDAY	TOTAL
MAIN TOWNS							N/A
HOTEL (attach SM's written OK)							
TRANSPORT (give journey details)							
PETROL (show p per litre)							
OIL							
TOLLS							
PARKING							
TELEPHONE CALLS (call-box only)							
POST/STAMPS (P.O. receipts attached)							
OTHER							
1							
2							
TOTALS							

Complete for Company or own car

Speedo Reading:
Previous Friday p.m..................
This Friday p.m..................
Total miles travelled..................

Note:

1. Attach VAT receipts for allclaims
2. Complete daily, mail each Friday to Head Office

SALES ADMIN USE ONLY
All receipts attached YES/NO

139

So much for expenses.

From the salesman's point of view, clearly defined objectives and controls will motivate him to meet or exceed those objectives and stay within the control parameters.

This can be good or bad.

If it lifts a salesman's performance it is good, if it makes a salesman complacent if he exceeds those objectives it is bad. So you must be extremely careful how you word sales reports or sales returns, to ensure that the minimum standards of performance required under the salesman's contract of employment do not figure as 'targets' against which performance is measured.

Obviously, the 'minimum standard' will be roughly average performance and this will be the standard you will expect from the conversion of cold calls into sales or the conversion of enquiries into sales, or the value of business obtained from existing customers, plus the generation of new accounts.

As we are now looking at controls, we need not look at the standards we expect, but simply at the methods we use to ensure that:

(a) The salesman puts in an honest week's work and
(b) We know what he has done.

Let us look at (a) an honest week's work.

I want to know how every hour has been spent on every day. I am looking at the performance of many salesmen so a deviation from the norm is easily identified.

At George Newnes, we were given a list of names to call on. The control was, you reported on the outcome of each call. If you made twenty calls, arranged seven appointments, gave four demonstrations and made one sale, you were working well. They needed no documentation other than the salesman's comments on the list of names and addresses they had given him.

At Gross Cash Registers, I built the sales force up to the ' 1600 retail outlet' level. We had no enquiries so the important thing was to ensure that these territories were worked methodically.

To me, this meant that they had to work to a plan geographically, ensuring that no potential customers were overlooked. So I introduced the Ordnance Survey map method of controlling the territory. I bought a complete set of Ordnance Survey maps and mounted them on the walls of each branch office around the country. I covered them with rigid, transparent, plastic film and, on the film, marked with chinagraph pencil the boundaries of each salesman's territory.

I knew that there were countless retail shops, pubs, garages, garden centres, working men's clubs, and other potential cash register users that were not to be found down the high street of the local shopping centre, and the only way to ensure that none was overlooked was to cover every highway and byway. Not only did this give us an opportunity to contact every potential customer, it meant that we would be calling on people who had never been called on by our competitors and never would be.

Coupled with the Ordnance Survey maps were 'scribble sheets'. I originally called them 'report sheets' but I found salesmen hated having to fill in a report sheet after every call, so I changed the name of the form to scribble sheet.

The idea was, and should still be, that the salesman should record the outcome of every contact, no matter how brief or inconsequential. The scribble sheet was designed to reduce the documentation to a minimum. Unless the salesman is required to report, no matter how briefly, on every call, how can you know for sure how many calls he has made?

You will see from the example of a scribble sheet, which covers one day or part of one day's work, that we can not only pick the district in which the salesman is working but any changes in district. We also have the name and address of each company called upon. We also know, by the ticks on the scribble sheet, if the call was a new call and, if so, was cold, by *d*irect *a*pproach (DA), the result of an enquiry or as a result of *p*ersonal *d*irect *m*ail (PDM).

If it was a call back, a tick will tell us so and if a sale resulted the type of sale will be recorded. If a sale did not result, the 'revisit' box will record the date for another visit. Unfortunately, these scribble sheets were often taken less than seriously.

Although they were designed to fold up into four so that they could

SCRIBBLE SHEET

Name........................ Branch................. PDM................. Date................. No. ....

District	Number and Street	Name	New			Call Back			Tel	DEM	Revisit	Type of Contract	Comments
			DA	ENQ	PDM	DA	ENQ	PDM					
FOR BRANCH MANAGER'S USE													

be carried in the salesman's inside jacket pocket with a cheque book or diary as a backing, some salesmen failed to fill them in on a call by call basis.

On Friday, they were required to attend the branch meeting at 3.30 p.m., when they would receive their salary and commission in respect of the previous week's work and they would also attend a branch meeting which was constructed to be educational and motivating, but before that they were required to report to their branch manager. On his wall was the Ordnance Survey map of the branch territory covered in plastic. Each salesman was required to mark on the map, in the colour of the month, the route he had taken that week by tracing it on the plastic, or by etching in areas he had worked that week.

When you put a salesman's worksheet on a map, you have a new dimension. Try it sometime.

If you have established, as you should, how many outlets there are in each of your sales territories and where they are, your salesmen's reports will tell you (a) that the demographic information you have is out of date (believe your salesmen) or (b) that his reports are unreliable.

If a salesman's reports do not reflect your own experience, or the 'norm', then you have got to prove him right or wrong.

I have not been averse to re-tracing a salesman's footsteps to see if his reports are true or false.

I have found them true. I have found them false.

But, above all, I have found that he has not put in a fair week's work. Obviously, everyone's definition of a fair week's work varies. I have good salesmen working for me today, who make twice as many calls as other good salesmen make. This does not necessarily mean that a salesman making fewer calls is not putting in a fair week's work. He may spend twice as long with each prospect and, by so doing, convert twice as many calls into sales.

Theoretically, the perfect salesman works from first light until midnight eight days a week, but the most valuable salesman is the one that produces the highest volume of the most profitable business. His report sheets will help you to identify the best method of spending each day subject, of course, to verification and recognition of the fact that every salesman is different and what suits Peter will not necessarily suit Paul.

Sometimes a company will have established a method of working that is enshrined in the salesman's job specification, based on the short-term experience of a sales manager who left his company many years ago. Somehow it has become folklore, a sacred cow that cannot be killed off in spite of the overwhelming evidence that this method of working does not suit the majority of successful salesmen.

I found in *every* company I joined that there was a formal induction course which told new recruits how to do their job, and what standards they were required to exceed to enjoy security of employment. In *every* company there were very successful managers and salesmen who said 'take no notice of what they tell you at head office, do it *this* way'.

If you have that situation in your company, then for goodness sake kill the sacred cows, listen to the sales force, read their call reports, understand what the successful salesmen are doing, and base your training and your salesman's job specification on today's successes, not on yesterday's sacred cows.

So the worksheet, the call report, the scribble sheet, call it what you will, will tell you two things:

1. Is the salesman putting in a fair week's work?
2. How the successful salesman allocates his time so that you will know how you should train others to emulate his example.

A brief summary which establishes his call pattern, his time allocation divided between research, telephoning, calling, re-visiting, is vital but not enough.

We need to know what happened on every meaningful contact if we are to ensure that no sale is lost through mismanagement, lack of relevant training, and support. Obviously, the importance of the contact report will vary from 'no importance' if you are selling £12 fire-extinguishers to private homes, to 'vital importance' if you are selling aircraft to airlines.

CONTACT REPORT							
	A/C No.	CONTACT (Tick)	EXEC. SEEN			CALL DATE	
NAME		I/VIEW	1	2	3		
No.		TEL.					
NAME OF COMPANY:							
STREET: ADDRESS:							
TOWN: POSTAL CODE:				TEL NO.			
EXEC. SEEN TODAY: NAME/TITLE:							

Call No.	1	2	3	other	Fixed callback date/time:	
(Tick)					Planned follow-up date:	

Interview results and follow-up action	Order details

Complete after every interview. Print clearly.
Continue overleaf.

The contact report is therefore a discretionary control document but, in my experience, if the sale is worth a salesman's weekly wage, I want to know what happened, what the next step is, and in the salesman's opinion, what chance there is that we will make a sale.

Facing the facts of life, salesmen leave, sometimes voluntarily but more often on request. When they leave, they may not feel the same affection for their employer that they felt on day one. Contact reports make it possible for the management to pick up the pieces and finalize promising business which the departing salesman has failed to close.

Contact reports with dates for callbacks, which should be 'closing calls', help you plan your schedule of field visits. If you know when a salesman has scheduled re-visits to important prospects you, as manager, are able to decide when and if you should accompany him.

They also give you an indication of the value of the business in the pipeline but, if you use contact reports or salesmen's forecasts as a basis for a sales forecast, it is essential to divide the salesman's forecast by two and advisable to divide it by four.

The information which can be gleaned from the basic control

documents makes it possible to identify training needs. It is sometimes difficult for a sales manager to extricate himself from beneath the rubble of sales administration, which may be compiled of recruitment procedures, termination procedures, customer demands, customer complaints, management demands, management complaints, and remember that his job is to increase sales and that sales training and sales support are his prime responsibility.

If you are controlling a fairly large sales force, you will not be controlling the salesmen yourself. You will have other managers which you may call branch managers or regional managers or field sales managers and they will control probably five or six salesmen each.

Obviously, just as they need to know what their salesmen are doing, you need to know what they are doing, but the control documentation you need from them must embrace not only what they are doing but what the salesmen under their control are doing.

The manager's weekly report that I introduced to Ansafone (see opposite) was a multi-purpose document, which enabled the branch manager to submit a report on every area of his responsibility on one piece of paper (other than his expense claim which he regarded as far more important). The detail of the form is now out of date, but the concept is still very valid.

It contained an analysis of each salesman's performance, taking into account his length of service.

It compared his cumulative annual rental business with quota, highlighting deficits.

It compared his annual rental business this week with weekly quota.

It examined the cold call 'direct approach' calls, demonstrations and contract performances. It examined the 'door drop' or distribution of direct mail literature by the salesman.

It examined the manner in which enquiries had been handled and the sales results therefrom.

It compared these results with minimum standards of performance which I had established based on the performance of the 'average' salesman.

It required the manager to declare the last date on which he had given field assistance.

Manager's Weekly Report. Week …

Name (enter total sales strength)	Date of joining	Cum AR Quota	Cum AR obtained	Cum deficit	Weekly AR Quota	AR this week	DA this week calls / dems / conts	Cum DA conts	DD this week sent / enqs / conts	Cum DD conts	Enqs. this week enqs / dems / conts	Cum enq conts	Cum enqs	Cum enqs conts	Tot conts	Min DA PDM	Min enq	Deficit	Date last cont	Date of last field assist.	Comments
TRG Wk. No…		Slimline 100 →																			
TRG Wk. No…		Slimline 100 →																			
TRG Wk. No…		Slimline 100 →																			
TRG Wk. No…		Slimline 100 →																			
TRG Wk. No…		Slimline 100 →																			
Unallocated																					
Others/OF																					
Totals																					

Additional comments

Contract analysis

Name				THIS WEEK							THIS YEAR						
	7	600	6A	6	100	CAP 1000	CAP 1400	7 Yrs	3 Yrs	1 Yr	BW	Purchase	7	600	6A	6	100	CAP 1000	CAP 1400	7 Yrs	3 Yrs	1 Yr	BW	Purchase
Unallocated																		
Total new																		
Old business																		

Details of branch meeting

Field assistance given this week (time/conts)

	Mon	Tue	Wed	Thu	Fri

Planned for next week (time)

	Mon	Tue	Wed	Thu	Fri

Special Report 1

Special Report 2

Negotiations for more this one machine

Company	No. M/Cs	Details
1		
2		
3		

The bottom half of the form was far from inquisitorial. Not only was each salesman's performance analysed by sales of each model this week and year to date, the manager had to declare how much time he had spent with each salesman on each day of the week and how much business had resulted in each day. He was also required to give a 'next week' activity forecast.

Without these basic controls, it is impossible to manage a sales force effectively.

Every company I know has a need for the basic controls I have defined plus a number of unique controls relevant to that business. One company I know requires its field managers to complete nine different control documents at the end of each month and ten at the end of each quarter.

It would take only a few days for someone who knew what he was doing to rationalize this documentation and, by so doing, reduce the amount of lost sales management time, which is devoted to completing these often repetitive and tautological returns.

You have to strike the right balance. You must not take away from the field manager the responsibility for completing control documentation. Nothing will bring home to him more forcibly his shortcomings and the shortcomings of his sales team than the recording in his own handwriting of results for the week, the month, the year, the way in which he has allocated his time over the past week, and the way in which he plans to allocate his time in the week to come.

These days, information technology can give management more information more quickly than ever before. Point of sale terminals provide retail store management with all the information they need on sales and stock control without a single till roll or stock check sheet being generated at the retail store. Obviously, till rolls are printed and stock checks are made for verification and security reasons, but the point I am making is that central management often do not need the information which local managers provide through control documentation.

Some field managers feel it is a waste of time to complete a control document that reports the value of sales achieved by each member of their sales team when head office already know what has been sold.

The sales have been reported to head office either by post, telephone, or data transmission. Obviously this is not always the case but, even when it is, the object of *control* documentation is to inform the person completing the document just as much as it is to inform the recipient.

The designer of control documentation must keep this thought uppermost in his mind.

Head office needs to know the value of sales. The control document needs to compare this level with quota or target on a man-by-man basis.

Head office needs to know how the manager has spent the past week or month, but the control document must highlight, for the field manager, the amount of assistance or training he has given to salesmen who need assistance or training, as evidenced by their sales results.

So control documents, whether completed by the salesman or his manager, perform several different functions:

1. They can act as constraints on wasteful expenditure of money and time.
2. They record events and provide an ongoing record that can be used to progress sales and maximize business.
3. They can act as a communication medium between salesman and manager, manager and head office.
4. They can identify training needs for the salesman.
5. They can identify training needs for the manager.
6. They impose a discipline upon everyone completing them to analyse their own performance so that they will know what to do to become more effective.

12

Management of territory

My first 'sales management' appointment was with George Newnes (Aust.) Pty Ltd, and I was told that I could recruit up to ten salesmen to sell *Pictorial Knowledge*, *Chambers Encyclopaedia*, and the *Chambers Twentieth Century Dictionary* (called the *New Elizabethan Dictionary* in these days) throughout the State of Victoria in Australia.

Another manager was also allowed to recruit up to ten men, but his men sold electrical engineers' reference books.

A third manager was allowed to recruit up to ten men to sell engineers' reference books.

The three of us went about our work recruiting and training salesmen, most of whom worked in Melbourne. There were plenty of people to call on in Melbourne and there was no real necessity to work the rest of the State although, occasionally, a salesman (like me) would set off up country to work the sheep stations in the Western District, the orchards near the Murray River, or the dairy farmers in Gippsland.

The problem for me was not the management of territory because there was plenty of it. It was recruiting successful salesmen.

It was a straight commission job, so if you recruited ten salesmen and only seven of them made sales the company did not suffer, even if the unsuccessful salesmen's families did. We were preoccupied with recruiting and training anyone who had a clean suit, a need for money, an honest face, and a good command of the Australian language.

We controlled the territory in a simple fashion. We employed pensioners to call on every household in a defined area to establish if they had school-age children. If they had, they were a prospect and their names were recorded. Over a period of time it would have been possible to have canvassed every street in Melbourne and the surrounding suburbs, but I did not stay there long enough for this to happen. I was there only three years.

We never canvassed the dozens of sizeable towns throughout the State. There was no effective management of territory.

After three years with George Newnes, I returned to England and, although they were kind enough to offer me a management post in North-West London, I declined their offer. I had had enough encyclopaedia selling to last me a lifetime.

Instead, I joined Hussmann British Refrigeration as a multiple accounts executive selling supermarket refrigeration to supermarket operators.

There were three of us in the multiple sales division and it was our responsibility to work a defined list of accounts which, during my five years with the company, was never updated. The division was never enlarged, nor contracted. The three of us did our best, with considerable success I may add, to sell our refrigerated display cabinets and coldrooms to the retailers on our multiple accounts list.

I was never aware of any conscious effort on the part of management to manage the territory, the potential customers.

I knew that I was a manager at heart, so I was on the lookout for a sales management opportunity. It came wrapped up in the *Daily Telegraph*, not fish and chips, but Beanstalk Shelving needed a sales manager. I applied and was given the job without any experience of sales management.

I inherited the remnants of a good sales force, a sales force that had taken Beanstalk to market leadership. The previous sales manager had taken Beanstalk to the cleaners, having left to start up a business in competition with Beanstalk, and had taken with him the cream of the Beanstalk sales force.

I concentrated on the development of a sales process that could be used to generate a high volume of business for each remaining member of the sales force (see *The Secrets of Successful Selling*). My efforts were successful and the company recovered from the serious blow it had received, but I knew nothing about the control of territory and, when I resigned due to an inextricable breakdown of 'marriage' between the managing director and myself, I was still thinking in terms of sales skills and closing ability, as the routes to increased profitability instead of effective management of territory.

After about fifteen months, I could stand Beanstalk no longer (it is probably the best company in the UK now) and I applied for the position of personal assistant to the sales director at Gross Cash Registers and I was appointed.

Gross Cash Registers Ltd were managed professionally. The product was basic but good and more sophisticated products were on the way. There was a sales force of some hundred men, but sales were not growing. They had stagnated.

I was required to generate growth.

The first thing I did was nothing to do with territory management but a lot to do with growth. I developed a better way of working and taught it to the existing sales force so that their performance was improved.

I could not see any other practical ways in which the sales performance of the salesmen could be improved, so I was forced to explore the possibility of increasing the size of the sales force.

As I have explained in Chapter 11, the size of the optimum territory could be determined by establishing the call rate of a salesman working properly. The frequency at which he should visit each type of potential customer is the only other piece of information you need. If the call rate is one hundred calls per week and you want him to call three times a year, his territory should contain 1600 potential customers. If you want him to call once a month, he needs a territory in which there are 450 potential customers. The controls I used, the scribble sheet and the Ordnance Survey maps, enabled me to manage each territory very effectively. We used a different colour chinagraph pencil for each month of the year so that we could see at a glance when a street had last been worked. If four months had elapsed, we cleaned off the chinagraph and that street, or that village, became virgin territory again.

One major problem was that one or two salesmen claimed they had worked their territory in far less time than I knew they needed to work it thoroughly. They claimed that they had not as many outlets as I had claimed were on their territory. These salesmen had to be trained how to work a territory thoroughly, how to find every prospect possible by practical example in the field, using the methods described in detail in *The Secrets of Successful Selling*.

I managed the territory to such a degree that we had 400 salesmen working, where 100 had worked before.

You can imagine the howls of protest that could be heard from all the salesmen whose territories were cut into quarters! You have to use discretion and diplomacy to achieve such a transformation and you cannot do it overnight. Obviously, it takes a long time, years in my experience, to build a sales force of 400 men plus 100 managers. Therefore, the reduction in territory size is an evolutionary rather than a revolutionary process.

The first step is to formulate the structure of the sales force that will obtain when the growth plan has been effected completely. In my case, with Gross, it meant that most territories would be divided into four.

The sales force of 100 men were told of the plan, informally, and therefore knew that there were to be some eighty promotion opportunities into branch and regional management. While this development was taking place, their territories were divided into four and they were given one quarter of their original territory as their new, exclusive territory, but were allowed shooting rights over three territories, so to all intents and purposes they still had their original territory.

When I had doubled the sales force, many of them had been promoted and others still had three-quarters of their original territory.

The new recruits had only one third as much. This gradual evolution, which took some four years to complete, taught me some very interesting and valuable lessons.

I found that as the salesman's territory was reduced in size, so his sales increased. He complained bitterly about losing territory, but received larger and larger commission cheques.

You must realize that the business was geared exclusively to 'cold canvass' business, no enquiries. So the salesman's earnings reflected two things:

1. The number of demonstrations he gave.
2. His conversion ratio of demonstrations to sales.

The number of demonstrations he gave reflected his persuasiveness, his persistence in the approach. When his territory was large he was not too worried if a prospect said 'Not interested' or 'Too busy' because there was a virtually inexhaustible supply of prospects to call on.

The salesman who worked Sussex, calling on a butcher's shop in Worthing, would be told 'We don't make any money here, all the old dears that come in here take five minutes to make up their minds if they want a lamb chop or two sausages, and another five minutes fumbling in their purses to find a few coppers to pay for it, and another five minutes telling you how much they used to pay for a chop before the war. You want to go into Brighton, that's where the money is.'

So the salesman would take their advice and go to Brighton.

It is true that business is better in Brighton than in Worthing so the rents and rates are much higher, the competition is keener, and margins are cut to the bone, particularly in butchers' shops.

'If you want to sell cash registers, you'd be better off going to Haywards Heath, Crawley, and places like that,' the Brighton butchers would say, so the salesman would head north for the Eldorado of Crawley.

He had plenty of territory, so what did it matter if Worthing and Brighton were no good.

When his territory was cut to a quarter the size, to 1600 retail outlets, he valued every one. When a shopkeeper said he was having a tough time he did not give in. He said 'Okay, so have a look at our latest thing in cash registers just for the interest. It costs nothing to look. I'll bring one in'. Once in, he had a very good chance of making a sale.

The effect on productivity was not dramatic, but significant. Not only did the salesmen become more persuasive, more persistent, but they gave more demonstrations which generated more sales. Furthermore, giving more demonstrations slowed them down so they made fewer calls per day, thereby burning up less territory. No matter how few calls a good salesman made, I never reduced the territory size below 1600 retail outlets.

The best laid schemes o' mice an' men gang aft a-gley or words to that effect.

Although I had designed the optimum sales force structure for Gross Cash Registers, I had not fully taken into account the fact that salesmen are not robots or puppets, but people, with widely varying dispositions, temperaments, character traits, strengths, weaknesses, pet hates, superstitions, and political persuasions.

I found that many just could not work methodically, mechanically coming out of one shop and going into the shop next door, and the one next door to that, no matter what type of shop it was. They tended to stand in the middle of the market square and prejudge their chances in every retail outlet. Some loved pubs and working men's clubs (I wonder why!), some hated them. Some loved grocers, some hated them. Some, in fact most of them, hated chemists' shops. So I found that, whereas I had given each salesman his fair share of 1600 outlets plus pubs and garages, not all the outlets were being worked.

I tried the psychological approach. I divided the potential market into two. The retailers with low average sale values, like newsagents, pubs, greengrocers and the like, and the high value or multiple purchase outlets, like grocers, chemists, garages, clothing and departmental stores. I then combined two territories, where appropriate, and told one salesman that he could only call on newsagents, pubs, greengrocers etc., and the other that he could only call on grocers, chemists and the like.

There is no doubt that the experiment, for that is what it turned out to be, was successful, because the salesman, being forbidden to call on half the outlets, made jolly sure he called on the rest. His opposite number did the same. So every outlet was approached with enthusiasm.

Unfortunately, the experiment was short-lived. There were very few adjoining territories where one salesman hated pubs and the other loved them, but it was an interesting exercise.

It made me very conscious of the different ways in which a sales force can be structured to ensure maximum penetration of a market and maximum exploitation of the potential in each territory. Originally, I had been structuring a sales force purely on a geographical basis.

Although we were selling nine different types of machine to some forty different types of retail outlet, I saw the problem to be solved as one of territory size – how large should the territory be for a salesman to maximize sales of nine different types of machine to some forty different types of retail outlet.

I moved forward tentatively into the recognition of the opportunities to increase sales by directing the sales force into different market segments.

I was later to identify the third method of 'territory management' which was to have different salesmen selling different products.

So, territory management becomes a complex subject. We start with the need to identify and quantify the total market and its segments. If we have a range of products or services to sell, we need to establish how many prospects there are for each product or service and where they are. We need to establish through practical field work how many prospects can be handled efficiently in a defined timespan for each product or service.

We must then decide on how to control the territory:

1. Do we divide the country into x segments, selling all products to all prospects?
2. Do we divide the country into x segments with the salesman in each segment selling one product to all prospects?

3. Do we divide the country into *x* segments with one salesman selling all products to one type of prospect?
4. Do we perm these three options to provide a multi-layer specialist sales force?

I finished up at Gross with the majority of the sales force operating under option (1), selling the whole range to every type of prospect, but I also invoked option (3) in that I built a 'licensed' trade team that did nothing other than sell the whole range of machines to the licensed trade (how naive can you be to assume they did nothing other than sell the whole range of machines to the licensed trade, they were paralytic most of the time).

I also identified that the larger multiple retailers were a market segment in their own right, so they had an exclusive and therefore despised team of multiple account executives that sold the whole range of machines to a limited segment of the market.

When I moved to Ansafone, I was in a totally different market.

The sales force was working enquiries. The enquiry flow reflected the effect of the company's advertising campaign. If they advertised in the *Evening Standard*, but not in the *Liverpool Echo*, you needed ten salesmen in London to handle the enquiries, but no one in Liverpool. It was actually worse than that, sometimes. We advertised on Thames Television (now Carlton) which generated a high volume of enquiries, but advertising on Granada produced very few. I do not know why.

We could not take extreme action to solve a short-term problem which may never recur. Temporary, emergency, firefighting action is all part of a normal sales force's responsibility, so if there was a flood of enquiries generated by an unexpected response to an advertising campaign, the sales force had to cope with it. But correct management of territory must take the long-term view.

Television advertising was, for us, a doubly interesting exercise. We would probably never have considered it a viable option had we not persuaded Thames to install 110 Ansafones on 100 telephone lines to handle telephone response from holiday brochure advertising.

The whole concept of direct response television advertising sprang from those small beginnings and, within the space of a few months, we had installed banks of machines for Thames, Southern, Westward, HTV, Anglia, ATV, Granada, Tyne Tees, Border, Scottish, and Grampian. We lost Yorkshire to one of our competitors. Once holiday advertising had been proved a success, the television company sales forces sold the 'instant response' idea to a wide range of advertisers with great success, and we climbed on the bandwagon that we had set rolling.

Within twenty-five seconds of the commercial giving the telephone number, 01-388-1122, all one hundred lines were busy, all one hundred Ansafones were recording the incoming orders or requests for brochures, and the other ten were ready to take over when the machines on the first ten lines were full.

Unfortunately, a small percentage of the population is mentally subnormal in that they derive pleasure from uttering obscenities when there is no risk of being punched in the mouth, or from writing vulgar graffiti in the privacy of a public lavatory behind a securely locked door.

The temptation to leave obscene messages on the Ansafone when invited to call proved too great for them to resist, so roughly one call in ten recorded messages was unfit for the girls who transcribed the tapes to hear. It was impossible to trace the offending callers, so Thames TV with the help of British Telecom designed a simple, ultimate deterrent. It consisted of a set of headphones, a microphone, and a switching device. A supervisor wore the headphones and switched from line to line, listening in on the public responding to the advertisements. As soon as she heard a 'heavy breather' on the line, she would say 'We have now identified the telephone from which you are calling. You will be contacted by the police shortly', or words to that effect. The regulars became less regular, because these pathetic people are cowards and would rather run than be caught.

You would think that in an 'enquiry flow' situation the management of territory would be simple, but I did not find it so.

As I have already explained, I like to establish the number of prospects, the conversion ratio of calls to sales, the optimum frequency of contact or 'journey time' and, from those basic facts, determine the optimum territory size. When you have an enquiry flow generated by advertising, how do you know that the 'territory' is being managed correctly? How do you know if there is a vast untapped market that has not been tapped because your advertising has not been seen by those potential customers?

How do you know if your advertising makes your potential customer respond?

I certainly did not know if the 'territory' at Ansafone was being managed correctly because the sales force were handling enquiries generated by title corners or 'earpieces' as they are known on the front or back pages of the 'serious' press and by *Yellow Pages* quarter columns. There were vast tracts of the country and huge segments of the population that did not read the 'serious' press. They certainly did not see our advertisements. Perhaps we should have advertised on page three of *The Sun*, but we did not.

You can see how difficult it is to establish that you are working a territory effectively if the salesmen are responding to enquiries generated by advertising that does not reach all your potential customers?

I knew that the sales force at Ansafone, responding to enquiries, were not working their territories effectively, so I had to develop the best method of working a territory and, from my experience of the territory, I did that. I took into account the fact that every salesman would receive enquiries, but that these should not represent the major source of his business. I instructed the sales force in the manner in which they should handle enquiries, when to do so disrupted their pre-arranged territory plan.

I live in the real world, like you do. When a salesman got an enquiry, he dropped everything and went for it. Quite right too. The territory plan went out of the window, and if a steady flow of enquiries came to that salesman the territory plan never came back in through the window, it was left outside to wither on the vine.

This really was a real problem, it may be a problem to you. Give a salesman enough enquiries to earn a living which matches his 'comfort level' and he will never work harder (no matter how much the territory is underworked).

Somehow or other, I had to prove to the sales force, salesmen and managers alike, that there was a fantastic sales potential, far greater than the response to our advertising would lead one to believe, waiting to be tapped. They were not only sceptical, but happy to earn a good living, keeping their wives and sweethearts (may they never meet) in comfort, nay luxury.

I had to prove to the sales force that they were standing on top of a gold mine and that the only reason they had not been earning a small fortune was that they were afraid of approaching businesses direct to make appointments.

I backed up my argument by employing a new salesman, who would not know that we received enquiries. He would be trained to work from cold canvass.

This was not unreasonable, because I had already developed a simple, reliable way of generating business and I knew from this practical experience that calling on businesses in the right way, using the right words, was not only effective, it was enjoyable. People were, generally speaking, happy to talk to you and, in many cases, interested to hear what you had to say. This was using the 'no briefcase, no manual' technique.

This salesman, Brian Rapp, was a success. In his first month he made three sales, in his second month four sales, in his fifth month five sales, and then – disaster! His manager decided he was being unfairly treated and gave him a few enquiries. In the next month, he made one sale from the enquiries he had been given, plus four from his own direct approach. In the next – he made two sales from the enquiries he had been given and three from direct approach. The following month, he made three sales from the enquiries he had been given and two from direct approach.

So you can see that it is infinitely simpler to manage territory if you do not have enquiries than if you do.

Until a couple of years ago, I had always managed territory by allocating a defined area of ground to a salesman and then monitoring his work so that I could be satisfied that he was working that territory effectively. There are, however, other ways of managing territory.

With Gross Cash Registers and Ansafone, our customer base was the one-man business and upwards. Many of our customers worked from home as insurance salesmen do.

If, on the other hand, you are selling exclusively to a definable segment of the business community, the territory can be managed differently.

I am currently managing a sales force that sells a service to organizations that spend over £30, 000 p . a. on telecommunications. There are not that many, maybe twenty thousand of them. To manage each territory, I have those 'prospects' on the computer and every contact is controlled and monitored. It is impossible for any mishandled contact to slip through unnoticed. Just as the optimum size of territory has to be determined, so does the optimum number of identified prospects per man have to be determined to ensure that each salesman contacts potential and existing clients at the correct, predetermined frequency, and with the required determination.

A salesman's territory is no different from the farm on which I started my working life. It is one of the basic components of wealth. The degree of skill in management of the land, the territory, will determine the return per acre. So do not overlook this vital sales management responsibility.

13

Growth

I spent a pleasant couple of days at a hotel in Brighton a few weeks ago. I was not alone.

My companions where fellow managers and we were there to examine in some detail the manner in which we were managing the business. We were able to concentrate our minds, away from the telephone, the morning post, the MD.

We are naturally a sales orientated company, so we think we are doing all we can to stimulate sales, but it is surprising, when you stand back and take a deep breath of sea air, how much you can see that was not visible in the day-to-day, reactive management environment of the office.

If you want to reassure yourself that you are doing all you can to lead your sales force to success, I advise you to 'go bush' with a small group of management colleagues and 'brainstorm'. Question every procedure that you follow, call on your past experience. What did you do in other companies? Call on the writings of others who can slant a ray of light on a problem from a different angle.

Meetings of this kind are not unlike meetings of Alcoholics Anonymous. No, I do not mean that to qualify for attendance you have to be an alcoholic, even if some people say sales management may well set you on the road to becoming one. What I do mean is that, for an Alcoholics Anonymous meeting to be of any value, each person attending has to admit they have a problem. They have to stand up and say 'My name is John. I am an alcoholic'.

How can you cure a problem if you do not admit the problem exists?

We held our two-day meeting because we wanted to find ways of improving our performance, ways of increasing sales. If we were admitting that there might be ways of increasing sales, what were we really saying?

We were saying that what we had been doing in the past might be wrong.

Can you see the similarity with Alcoholics Anonymous?

We had to stand up and say 'My name is John. What I am doing is wrong'.

If there is a difference between an AA meeting and our meeting it is that the alcoholic knows the cure to his problem, even if it is incredibly difficult for him to implement it even on a one-day-at-a-time basis. We did not know the cure to our problem, which was slow growth.

I am not going to tell you what happened during those two days because it is company confidential, but this problem of slow growth, or even no growth, is very common, even if companies have good products and the market for them is healthy.

One of the reasons I found when I joined companies with growth problems was that the managers were not prepared to stand up and say 'My name is John and what I am doing is wrong'. It was quite obvious that what they were doing was wrong, because they had in the past grown to a profitable level but now they had plateaued, growth had ceased. Most probably the policies that they had defined some years ago were right at that time and had therefore led to growth. But the growth had stopped. They were not prepared to accept that their policies were now out of date, because those policies had become sacred cows.

'We have always done it this way. This way has always proved effective and we are not prepared to slaughter this sacred cow.'

The only reason I had been brought into these companies was because the incumbent sales management was no longer leading the company to market leadership. They had run out of ideas. The shareholders wanted to bring a fresh mind to bear on their problems.

It is so much easier for an outsider, who knows what he is doing, to say 'What you are doing is wrong', than it is for the person who conceived and gave birth to the sacred calf to say 'My sacred cow should be slaughtered'.

This does not mean that the only cure for lagging sales is to bring in an outsider and get rid of the existing sales management.

On the contrary, it means that to be an effective sales manager you have to generate growth. To generate growth, you not only have to *define* the policy, you have to *update* it constantly by questioning its validity and by injecting new ideas, which must be tried and tested, adopted or rejected.

Probably the most important responsibility of a sales manager is to establish in most meticulous detail everything the average recruit should do to generate a profitable level of sales and then train him to achieve that objective.

Each time I joined a new company that was floundering, I put myself through the induction and training programme. I sat in with new recruits and I absorbed the training, probably better than they did.

I then went out selling on my own to see how well I would perform if I were an average salesman doing what I had been taught to do.

I am not an average salesman, I am an above-average salesman, and I found that I was struggling to meet the company's minimum standards of performance.

Because I had not been the one who had defined the sales methods that new recruits were required to adopt, it was not difficult for me to look objectively at what was being taught, and judge how effective that teaching was when put into practice in the field.

Not only would it be impossible for the existing sales management to look at the problem as objectively as I could, because they had created the problem, but they did not always go out selling with the new recruits to see how difficult it was for them to make sales using the methods that were being taught.

Naturally, there were successful salesmen, salesmen who had been with the company for a long time, salesmen who were keeping the company afloat. I went out with them. By combining their successful sales experience with my own successful sales experience I developed a method of training the average new recruit so that he would generate a profitable level of business in an acceptable period of time.

To be successful as a sales manager, you must not only be prepared to stand back and question everything you do, but you must be able to find the answers to problems. You must be prepared to spend a lot of time in the field with your sales force and on your own, so that you keep in touch with the market and can redefine your sales training programme to reflect the performance of your successful salesmen and your own experience in the field.

It is not only 'in the field', if that expression means 'in front of the prospective customer' . You have to detail every action the salesman must take to be successful, as well as every action you or his manager must take to ensure his success, from start to finish.

I knew it was my responsibility to develop the sales process that would be the fundamental fulcrum of 'the numbers game'.

What do I mean by 'the numbers game'?

I mean that the average salesman following company policy will make 'so many' calls, physical or by telephone, which will lead to 'so many' sales interviews which will lead to 'so many' sales of £x value. The significance of this is that if you know that if Mr Average makes 'so many' calls which lead to 'so many' sales interviews which lead to 'so many' sales of £x value, all you have to do is recruit extra average salesmen.

No?

No, not quite so simple. What I found in practice, was this. You have to develop on your own, in the field, a method of selling which you find easy and profitable and then prove that other people – the Mr

Averages of this world – can also be successful using the new methods that you have developed.

I adopted a salesman who was about to be dismissed for poor sales results. I took him under my wing and I taught him my new method of working. I worked with him in the field and within a week he was producing three times his previous results, well above average performance, a significant achievement. But I could not retrain every salesman, so I had another hurdle to jump. I had to prove, first, that a branch manager., retrained by me, could be successful, and second, that he could then teach the new method to the salesmen in his team so that they became more successful.

I have been through this same procedure in each of the companies I have worked with, but there is no doubt that one of the most effective and profitable changes I introduced was with Gross Cash Registers. Not surprisingly, before my arrival on the scene, the salesmen had been approaching shopkeepers extolling the virtues of cash registers in general and Gross Cash Registers in particular. At the suggestion of the then sales director, Sydney Downton, I set about developing an approach which had an adding machine (calculators had not yet been invented!) as the focus of attention.

It sounds almost incredible today, but we were able to introduce a simple one-memory adding machine, which cost £50, into simple retail outlets where the often elderly proprietor had great difficulty in 'doing the books' at the weekend.

We also sold adding machines of various sizes to postmasters, who had a great deal of adding up to do after they had closed for the night.

But the real significance of this change of approach was the effect it had on normal retail outlets. Their minds were geared to sales 'over the counter'. Self service was not commonplace then. They knew that there was a real risk of errors in addition when one customer bought a number of different items. We gleaned all the evidence we could, from trade sources, that errors in addition were common. It was powerful ammunition. It seems incredible today, in the age of the electronic point-of-sale data collection terminal, that until only comparatively recently grocers were writing down on the side of a 2 Lb packet of sugar, the price of every item the customer had purchased, were adding them up in their head and forgetting to include the price of the packet of sugar! But they were.

Shopkeepers were attracted to this idea of using an adding machine to add up the different items that a customer had bought but they said 'But there's nowhere to put the money, is there?'

This led us in to the itemizing cash register which is today as common as the pocket calculator, but in those days it was state of the art technology, an investment of £200 – about £1,000 today.

If you can develop a method of working that increases even one new recruit's performance by 300 per cent you are on to a winner. I knew that I was.

I went to see our Reading branch manager, Maurice Crowcombe, who tragically died of a heart attack some years go. He was ambitious, he was competitive, and hungry. I went out cold canvassing with him and I did all the work. The approach was simple. I went up to the nearest member of the staff and said 'Good morning. You are the proprietor, I presume'.

This generated one of four responses:

1. Yes.
2. No. He is the man over there in the white coat.
3. No. He is out at the moment.
4. No. We are only a branch office. Our head office is at . . .

These were four positive replies which either confirmed that we were speaking to the proprietor or which pointed us in the right direction. I never said 'Are you the proprietor?' or 'May I speak to the proprietor?' or 'Can you tell me where I can contact the proprietor?' or 'Can you give me the name of the proprietor?' for all are clumsy ineptitudes.

When I found that I was speaking to the proprietor, I said 'My name is Adams of Gross Cash Registers, although this is not why I have called to see you today.'

(There is no answer to that.) 'We've noticed in our travels that a great many people are using an adding machine, either on the counter or behind the scenes somewhere, and as we don't make an adding machine ourselves we have taken on the agency for the Burroughs machine.' (At this point I would take the machine from under my arm, remove the cover and place it on the prospect's counter and say 'Have you seen this one before?')

Normally they had not 'seen this one before' so I continued 'Well, the beauty of this machine is that it is so easy to use. If you want to record sixpence you press 6, if you want to record one shilling and sixpence you press 1 and 6, and if you want to record one pound, two shillings and sixpence you press 1, 2 and 6, and to add them all up you press Total. Easy?'

You will realize that this was prior to decimalization of the currency in 1971 and that, with an adding machine, unlike a calculator, you had to pull the handle on the side of the machine between each entry.

I am describing this approach in detail because I want to illustrate the degree of detail I believe it is necessary for the sales manager to define if he is to be sure of achieving controlled growth that can be budgeted.

I would not allow a salesman to key in different amounts of money, for whereas he knew that when he totalled the items entered in the keyboard, the printed total should be £1. 4. 6d and he could check that he had operated the machine correctly, were he to key in unfamiliar amounts the total would also be unfamiliar and an error would not be immediately apparent.

Obviously this change in the method of working was highly successful, otherwise I would not be telling you about it. Not only did it enable us to sell many more cash registers, not only did it reduce the number of salesmen who failed, but it gave us the valuable revenue derived from the sales of 800 adding machines per month. We sold more Burroughs adding machines than any other organization in the world.

If you are going to define the sales process in detail, it is not just the method of approach you have to worry about, it is the lot. You have to put theory into practice. We all know that you must not sell features; you have to sell benefits. We have all stood up in front of our salesmen and have explained the difference. Maybe we have gone one step further and taught our salesmen that, first of all, you have to lay the foundation for the benefit, identify the *need* before you can sell a benefit that fills a need, but to ensure the success of Mr Average you must give him the exact words to use, instruct him, teach him, train him.

It is the same at the close.

To ensure growth, you must define in meticulous detail the manner in which the average recruit must sell so that you can recruit, in confidence, knowing that the average recruit will succeed and be profitable.

When I was confident that the new method of working was not only successful for me but that I could teach a salesman how to be successful and that another manager could teach his salesmen the new methods, I held a meeting of all the branch managers. I explained to them what I had been doing and I gave them factual evidence of the improvement in performance that had been achieved. I converted this into the increases in earnings it represented for managers and salesmen alike.

Maurice Crowcombe – a fellow manager – confirmed that he had been successful and had retrained his salesmen successfully so that they saw that if he had been successful they also should be successful. There were joint sales managers at Gross, John Cherry in the north and Harry Bloom in the south. I introduced them to the new method and they, in their turn, trained the other managers.

The managers then retrained the sales force and, as you would imagine, some were very successful and some were not, but overall the exercise was a resounding success.

I then introduced the 'average concept'.

If you have a sales force of ten, then your sales are ten times the average. If you have a sales force of a thousand, your sales are one thousand times the average. Therefore, one of the most important and critical factors in lifting a sales force that is using an effective method of selling the product or service, is to raise the value of the average. Obviously, I used the conventional methods of increasing sales through training and motivation, but I also used a far more effective technique. I divided the total sales revenue by the number of sales people employed and came up with an average, the figure I call, amazingly, the magical average.

I found this a magical formula for, whereas most companies sack people who produce *below quota*, I found that if I sacked people who produced *below average* I had a permanent ongoing basis for recruitment. Every time I replaced a salesman with someone better, I increased the average. I never reached a situation where everyone was exceeding quota and we would have plateaued.

I am sure that those of you who are experienced sales managers will be thinking to yourselves there is no guarantee that if you sack a sub-average salesman, you will recruit an above-average salesman in his place, and that is absolutely true. I have recruited thousands of salesmen over the years, and I have devoted a great deal of time and thought towards perfecting recruitment techniques that will reduce the risk of employing unsuitable applicants. I have tried to identify the specific characteristics and personality traits that successful salesmen possess. I have employed industrial psychologists to advise me, but whatever route I followed, my success rate was 50 per cent. Half of my recruits were better than the people they replaced and therefore increased the 'average' and half were not and did not. I therefore knew that if I had a salesman who did not respond to training and who was producing well below the average, I had to replace him, and the probability was that I would have to recruit twice to recruit someone better.

But when I did recruit someone better, they increased the average and brought a whole new trawl of below-average performers under the microscope.

It was then that I realized that the worst thing any company can have is a stable sales force. Without the injection of new talent the average will not increase substantially. New records will not be set, and do not underestimate the setting of new records, new standards. It can become a mania. I have seen records increased by 300 per cent.

Although dramatic improvements can be obtained through the introduction of more effective sales methods and the replacement of sub-average performers, it is impossible to achieve substantial growth unless the sales force is enlarged. Although this is without doubt the most difficult aspect of growth, it is the most important.

You will not find companies like IBM, 3M, or Beechams with only a handful of salesmen. So you have to accept, as I did, that if you are going to build sales performance, company turnover by a factor of 2, 4, 6, 8, or 10, you will have to build the sales force in numbers. There is no other way growth of this magnitude can be achieved.

I faced the problem and it brought me into the long-term planning stage.

What was the correct size of the sales force? Obviously, a sales force of two was too small, a sales force of 20,000 too large.

At Gross Cash Registers, we were selling to retail outlets and it was comparatively easy, with the help of the market research companies, to determine not only how many retail outlets there were but where they were. Because I had developed the sales methods myself, I knew as a matter of fact how many calls a day a salesman could make, how many sales per week he should make, and how frequently he should revisit to ensure that he did not miss any sales opportunities.

I concluded that a salesman needed 1600 retail outlets plus garages and the licensed trade to enable him to call on each prospect three times per year and produce above-average performance for the foreseeable future. That meant making 25-40 calls per day and I knew that that was realistic because I had done it myself.

This meant that I needed 400 salesmen working 400 territories.

I had, at that time, about 100 salesmen, many of whom were below average. When you come to the conclusion that you need 400 average salesmen it raises all kinds of problems.

People are people. They are not pawns, bishops, and knights on a chessboard. You cannot deliberate and then move them in the most logical manner to 'checkmate'.

This did not deter me from defining the long-term objective of a sales force of 400 salesmen, with 80 branch managers and 20 divisional managers, which I achieved according to plan. The plan took into account the need to recruit twice to find one good employee (and that is what we had to do). It also took into account the resistance we would experience from the existing sales force, which could see their territories being reduced to one quarter their present size.

I did reduce their territories to one quarter of their present size, but I like to think that I did it painlessly.

I divided the country into 400 territories with an approximately equal number of retail outlets (excluding multiples) in each territory.

I gave each of the existing sales force exclusive rights over approximately one quarter of his previous territory and shooting rights over the other three-quarters, which represented another three new territories. As new salesmen were appointed, they were given one of the new territories and the established salesmen had the size of their territory reduced by one quarter.

Before you start feeling sorry for the poor salesmen whose territory was being reduced by the incursion of the new recruit, let me tell you that the value of business being obtained by the sales force was greater from the new, small territories than it was from the large territories that remained. They were spending less time travelling and were therefore spending more time selling. They were spending less on petrol and what was infinitely more important they placed a much higher value on each prospect. I have explained this phenomenon in Chapter 12, but I did not then elaborate on the beneficial side effects.

If you have a competent salesman calling regularly on all the prospects on his territory, it is almost certain that he, and that means *your* company, is the one your prospects consider to be the market leader. No other company in your industry puts their name in front of each prospect as frequently and as effectively as you do.

I remember my boss, Sydney Downton, at Gross Cash Registers, saying 'If all we did was walk into every shop once a month and say "Gross Cash Registers are the best cash registers in the world" within six months every retailer would believe it and would choose Gross next time they bought a new cash register.'

Obviously, he was right. Dr Goebbels was right. He said 'If you say something three times, people will believe it is true.'

I have never been involved in selling consumables, but I know that the mention of a new type of potato crisp once a year will not tempt you to change from your favourite brand. But a concentrated promotion on television, well executed, will convince you that you should buy some of these new crisps 'They must be good, they are so well known.'

There were many competitors in the cash register business. NCR were the market leader from 1890 to 1965. There were other cash registers with a substantial hold on the market, such as Sweda, Hassler, Hugin, Anchor, Gledhill, Regna, and others. We became the market leader in the late 1960s, not because our cash registers were dramatically better than our competitors, not because our cash registers were dramatically cheaper than our competitors, but because none of our competitors had 400 salesmen, each with 1600 retail outlets calling on every one of them at least three times a year, telling them that they should trade out their old machine for a new Gross machine or telling them why they needed to buy their first cash register.

Exactly the same principle applied with Ansafone. Our name appeared on the front or back of every serious newspaper at least once a week. The name Ansafone became the generic term for a telephone answering machine. I had 100 salesmen delivering 125 pieces of promotional literature to business people every week. 12,500 every week. 650,000 every year. On top of that, 100 salesmen were making an average of thirty cold calls per day, 150 per week. Each M 5,000 per week as a sales force, 785,000 calls per year. Was it surprising that when people thought of telephone answering machines they thought of Ansafone?

I have learned that concentration of sales activity does not reduce the effectiveness of the individual salesman, it increases it.

I do not want to imply that before I joined these companies they were not trying to increase the size of their sales forces, because they were. The problem was, they did not know how to do it. I remember one manager in the Midlands who was recruiting six men at a time and they all failed.

I worked the other way.

I wanted more managers because the more managers you have the more people you can recruit, train, and motivate at the same time.

Obviously there were problems to overcome. I have already explained how the territory size problem solved itself, but if you increase the number of teams or branches, you will sometimes find yourself with an under-strength branch which is uneconomic. It is not only uneconomic for the company, it is uneconomic for the manager. As you already know, I had established that the ideal branch consisted of a manager and five salesmen. This meant that he could spend time with every member of the branch each week, even if he did not spend a full day with the established, mature members. He would have no difficulty in reaching branch quota and thereby earn a good living.

If, on the other hand, he found himself with only three salesmen, then he was still required to achieve branch quota to generate a satisfactory level of profitability for the company and for himself. He was in this circumstance, required to work for three days with his three salesmen and two days on his own, generating business.

He was not paid the high salesman's commission on his own sales for this would have encouraged him to sell on his own rather than spend time training his salesmen, but it meant that his override commission on the branch turnover was inflated by his own efforts.

Recruiting additional salesmen highlighted the need for a long-term plan. I realized very soon that I could not go on recruiting salesmen without having established the manner in which they would be trained and managed.

The first principle I accepted was that one manager can only train one new salesman at a time.

The second principle I accepted was that a branch manager was at his optimum with five salesmen, but could operate effectively with four or six.

These principles were based on my own findings from trial and error. Based on these principles, I started to increase the size of the sales force by recruiting new sales people and by progressively promoting experienced salesmen into management.

This process is illustrated below, starting with a basic sales force of thirteen people comprising a sales manager, two branch managers and ten salesmen.

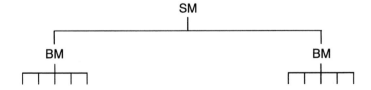

The first step is to recruit three new salesmen and attach one to each branch and one to the sales manager for training. We now have thirteen salesmen.

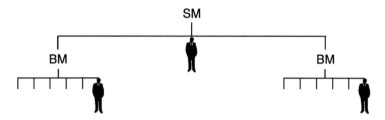

This may require two intakes for, as I have explained, recruitment is seldom 100 per cent successful.

The next step is to promote one of the most experienced salesmen to branch management, create a third branch and recruit three more salesmen.

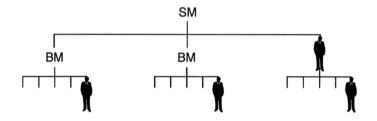

We then move on to the next step, which is to recruit another three salesmen, thereby bringing the strength of each branch up to six.

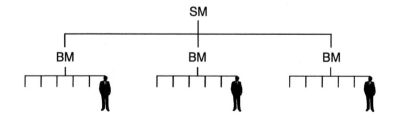

The fourth step is to promote another salesman, thereby bringing the number of branches up to four and to recruit another four salesmen.

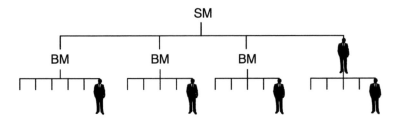

Step number five is to promote another salesman to branch management and recruit another five new salesmen.

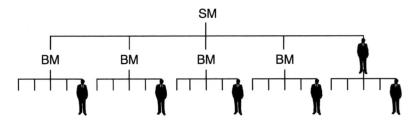

You will notice that every time we increase the number of managers we can increase the number of salesmen recruited at one time.

So, the original sales force of thirteen men has now become thirty-one. The more critical factor, however, is that the number of branch managers being controlled by the sales manager is five. I had already established that the optimum number of salesmen that a branch manager could manage was five, but he could manage six. I therefore assumed that a sales manager could control up to six branch managers.

Experience proved me wrong. Maximum effectiveness was with three or four. It was therefore obvious that I needed an additional layer of management if I were to achieve sustained growth.

I introduced regional managers at this stage to control three or four branches. This entailed promoting two branch managers to regional status and three salesmen to branch managers. Two of them filled the vacancies left through promotion and the third was to create a sixth branch. This made it possible to recruit six new salesmen and still have effective management control.

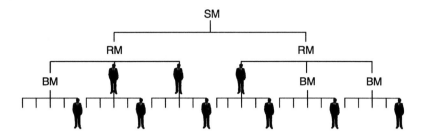

Actually, that is not completely true. Just as it is impossible to be 100 per cent successful when recruiting salesmen, so it is impossible to be 100 per cent successful when promoting salesmen into management.

Good salesmen are potentially good managers, for they have the ability to get people to do what they want them to do, and that is half the battle in management. The other half required training, but training in what? Obviously, detailed job specifications were needed for branch and regional managers, on which a training programme could be based.

I produced those job specifications and then set about producing a set of management notes with supporting documentation where necessary for each area of responsibility.

Obviously, the final objective for the branch manager was to produce a full complement of successful salesmen. The definition of 'successful salesman' was a moving target because as overall standards improved the value of average performance increased. But it was not only the value of business written on which a salesman's performance was assessed, his ability to document sales accurately and to complete those reports which the company required was also important, sometimes even more important. I have known a high volume of business from one salesman turn out to be less profitable than lower performance from another salesman due to the problems generated by poor documentation and administration.

The branch manager must therefore be accomplished in all aspects of the salesman's job and must perform in accordance with the salesman's job specification in this respect, as well as his own.

14

Motivation

Motivate: to provide with a motive*
Motive: an incitement of the will*
Motivation: motivating force, incentive*

(*Source: Chambers Twentieth Century Dictionary.)

It is easy to outline a training programme and comparatively easy to teach an intelligent person how to do the job. Whether or not they become consistent salesmen is another matter.

Whereas many managers and many companies accept that it is their responsibility to teach the sales force how to do their job and to provide the necessary administrative support, they do not realize that it is also their responsibility to see that their salesmen devote enough of their time, their effort, and their emotions to being consistently successful.

I learned that motivation was more important than anything else. No one will deny that.

There are many people who know what they want in life and go after it. It is called ambition.

Some want political power.

Some want to be millionaires.

Some want to discover a cure for cancer.

Some want to play Hamlet.

I suppose I had an ambition, but I think that is too grand a name for it. As a sales director I had a goal. My goal was to increase sales turnover and profitability month after month after month. Boring is it not? But, because I had the ambition to makes sales grow I devoted a great deal of time, effort, and emotion towards the achievement of that goal. I did more than teach and provide administrative support, I created an environment in which many members of the sales force could realize their ambitions.

Naturally, some of them had simple ambitions like 'being promoted into management'. As I was building a sales force, the opportunities for promotion were very real and these people were therefore naturally motivated to generate a high volume of sales over a fairly long period of time which, with a modest amount of forelock tugging and boot-licking, would virtually guarantee promotion.

Obviously, the opportunities for promotion could not qualify as a motivator if the company was not expanding. So I had a chicken and egg situation. Fortunately, I was able to generate expansion by improving the effectiveness of the sales force, and therefore there were always several opportunities for promotion, not only from salesmen to branch manager, but also from branch to regional management.

Obviously, the desire for promotion is not the only 'motivator' but before we look at motivation in detail, let us consider when we should use motivation as the most appropriate management tool and when we should not.

Let us look at three categories of potentially successful salesmen:

1. The man who learns quickly and develops into a successful salesman, with normal training and handling.

2. The man who makes slow progress but of whom we feel 'he has all the qualities needed to be successful'.
3. The man who has been successful during his initial training, or for a longer period, but who starts to decline in effectiveness.

Obviously, the first category – the successful man causes us no concern as long as he continues to perform, but we have to be sure that we create a climate in which he will continue to succeed.

The second category often has the ability to succeed but not the will. In this case, we have to develop his desire to succeed.

In the third category, the experienced man has lost interest in the job for one of many reasons and we have to find out why and cure the problem.

In all these cases I am pre-supposing that the problem is not one of sales training, but of management, for in sales management we have the dual responsibility of teaching a man *how* to do the job and then making him *do* it.

Making him *do* it is often called 'motivation' so I will use this word, but I will define it as 'harnessing the ambitions of others to achieve mutual gratification'.

Now, you may think that this definition has all kinds of X-certificate overtones, reminiscent of Hollywood film producers using the casting couch, but that is not what I mean.

I know that you will not get people to do what you want them to do unless *they* want to do it. So you have to discover the ambitions of others and then channel their energy into fulfilling that ambition, while at the same time generating for you the volume of business you require. Hence the mutual gratification.

The fascinating thing about motivation is that it is different for every single salesman. You can have a standard sales training policy, a scripted presentation, a proven method of closing sales which, if used correctly, will be effective for everyone. You can insist upon compliance and justifiably rebuke anyone who deviates from this proven method of selling your product or service because it is *proven*. But motivation is something else.

Motivation is personal, it is peculiar to the individual. What turns one salesman on turns another off. It is the challenge that sales managers must face, and their ability to motivate each individual member of their sales force on an individual basis will determine whether they are a grade A, grade B, or grade C manager.

Let us look at the three different types of potentially successful salesmen we have identified.

They all have the ability to succeed but need effective management to achieve and sustain their potential.

We need to establish his medium- and long-term goals, and this is where sales management is dramatically different from factory management. In factory management you generate good working conditions, good canteen facilities, muzak, wages not less than competitors in the same town, and efficient training in the necessary skills.

Employees will be clocked in and out and their production will be measured, and they will either remain employed or become a monthly statistic published by the Department of Unemployment.

Sales management is not like that. You have to get to know each salesman and recognize that unique individual who can sell consistently. You need to take time out to get to know him, and his partner, if he has one.

So successful salesmen may not continue to be unless we know what makes them tick. I know that I have a far better chance of finding out what makes them tick if I talk with them *and* preferably their partner.

Sometimes you will find that the salesman who learns quickly and develops into a successful salesman has the 'management ambition', and unless he sees opportunities for promotion he will become restless and will again start reading the 'situations vacant' columns in the newspapers.

To 'motivate' this man, you need to establish, as exactly as possible, the performance level he would have to sustain over a defined period of time to qualify for promotion. I know that, in the overwhelming majority of situations, this may not be possible, so a compromise may have to be reached. Ask yourself 'Why does he want promotion into management?'

You will not be able to answer, but *he* can.

Is it for the money?

Is it for the kudos?

Is it because he regards it as the first rung on the ladder to senior management?

Is it because he wants to teach others?

Is it because he wants to park a better car than his neighbour's in his driveway?

Unless you can get to know him well, you will not discover the true ambition that is hidden behind the publicly proclaimed one. If you can offer this paragon of virtue promotion, you will either string him along for as long as possible, benefiting from his consistent sales performance or promote him quickly, dependent on how desperate you are for managers. Either way, you have motivated him and retained him as a happy and profitable employee. But, if promotional opportunities are few and far between and there is a real possibility that he will develop senile dementia before his promotion comes through, then you must look for other ways to motivate him.

Suppose he wants promotion for the money, not the kudos, nor for career advancement.

In *all* the companies I have worked for the front-line managers earn less than the top-line salesmen. This is because the front-line managers are paid an override commission on the team performance and their scale of commission is structured so that if every member of the team produces 100 per cent quota performances, the managers earn more than the average salesman. If, on the other hand, the salesmen's performances vary equally from 50 per cent quota to 150 per cent quota, so that the average performance is 100 per cent, the earnings of the 150 per cent salesman is higher than his manager's.

If you are going to pay people on a performance-related basis, this apparent anomaly cannot be avoided. I, as a manager, totally accept it because, although it may seem illogical that I as a manager may earn less than a member of my sales force, the fluctuations in my income are minimal because, even if I am lying in bed with a temperature, under my doctor, I am still earning commission on the sales achieved by all the healthy members of my sales force.

The sick salesman, on the other hand, is not only in bed he is in financial trouble.

If a top-flight salesman's ambition is promotion because he thinks he will then earn more money, he should be told the facts of life. The average manager will not earn as much as his top salesman, not only in this company but in any company that remunerates its sales staff on results.

Is it for the kudos? If you know a Greek scholar, he will tell you that 'kudos' is a Greek word meaning credit, fame, renown, or prestige.

There are many ways in which your gem of a salesman can enjoy kudos.

One simple way is to publish a weekly report of achievements. The structure and content of this report must be carefully considered for *every issue*. On no account must a member of the sales office staff be given the *job* of compiling and distributing a weekly bulletin of sales or contest performances.

The effect the weekly bulletin has can be dramatic. If it has been a bad week and half the sales force has sold nothing, then under no circumstances must the results of the bottom half of the sales force be published. The bulletin must be much like a newspaper.

The national press do not divide the front page into four and report politics in one quarter, finance in another, gossip in the third quarter, and sport on the fourth. They allocate space to reflect the importance (in the editor's opinion) of the events of the previous day. On one day, the whole of the front page is devoted to an air crash. On another it is split between Edwina Currie criticizing Northerners for being overweight, and the interception of a boatload of cocaine in West Wales.

The weekly sales bulletin should be just as flexible.

Whereas I believe implicitly that sales management must not only be scrupulously fair, but must be seen to be scrupulously fair. I think there must be a degree of discrimination when deciding what the management must be fair about.

If being fair means giving everyone of equal merit equal recognition, equal reward, equal praise, then I agree.

If it means giving everyone, regardless of merit, regardless of effort, regardless of performance, equal recognition, then I disagree.

So the bulletin must always strive to 'motivate', i.e. give recognition to those members of the sales force who deserve recognition and, where possible, omit totally any reference to those who fail to produce a creditable level of business, although there are occasions when their results, without comment, presented to the public, will subsequently shame them into producing a satisfactory level of business.

If we are going to motivate the salesman who wants the respect of his peers (kudos), then we must try to include his name, in a favourable light, in as many bulletins as possible. Obviously, if he is a good salesman, his name will appear naturally, but if it does not because he has had a bad week, then engineer some honest figures that will show that, although he has had a bad week this week, over the past x weeks his performance has been outstanding.

Even if his performance over x weeks has been outstanding and this fact is stated in the bulletin, you must remember that the whole object of 'motivation' is to get everyone performing at a high level and that is not what 'Chummy' is doing at the moment. If he is motivated by kudos, then it is equally possible that he will work hard to ensure that he does not lose the respect he has earned.

It is not at all out of place to say in a bulletin 'Sue Perior, who has been one of the most consistent sales people this year, has had a rare blank week this week, which has allowed Jim Nastik to overtake her. But watch this space, because if she runs true to form she will be back in the lead next week'.

I remember telling one of my managing directors that on no account should he include in his weekly newsletters any information of importance or any instruction upon which the sales force were required to act. He was quite nonplussed, 'Why do you say that?' he asked.

I mentally bought the *Daily Telegraph* and started reading the 'Situations Vacant' columns before I said 'Because they don't read them'.

He found it very difficult to accept that the lyrical prose which he wrote sitting in his garden or his drawing room each Sunday afternoon was promptly consigned to the waste paper bin each Tuesday. But it was. Not only were his essays boring, he never mentioned the names of any members of the sales force, there was nothing in there with which they could identify.

Most people enjoy seeing their name in print. God knows why. If you, or one of your children, are mentioned in the local paper you buy more than one copy. If there is a photograph, you buy five!

If salesmen know they may well be mentioned in the weekly sales letter or bulletin, they will read it every week to see if they are mentioned, if for nothing else. So, the secret is to mention as many members of the sales force as possible as often as possible.

'Brighton branch under the individual, nay singular but singularly successful management of Abel Seaman, are again well up in the ratings this week.

'Much of the credit must go to newcomers Peter Doubt and Mark In time, who both made their first sales this week. Well done, Peter and Mark.

'As you would expect, the bulk of the business came from the anchor men Lou Tennant and Reg Ister, who took over the mantle from Pat Riarch and Bill Board, who did so well last week. Sam Browne did not score this week, but his polished performances will get him back into the charts next week for sure.'

If you appreciate good journalism you are probably, by now, on the way to the loo to throw up. But, believe me, if you want to motivate salesmen you cannot do better than mention as many members of the sales force as possible as often as possible in a weekly bulletin. Even the low producers can be stimulated into action by praise.

I am sure you have heard of the power of suggestion. If you conspire with others to tell someone they look ill, the constant reference to their appearance *will* make them ill. Conversely, praise can give confidence which breeds success.

Weekly bulletins which give regular recognition to the worthy achievers are like saline drips. They prevent the living from dying.

They do not stimulate activity like the injection of adrenalin into the bloodstream and this we have to do from time to time if we are to maximize performance, set new standards, and give the high producers that extra stimulus that will keep them competing with each other.

A competition can be the enzyme that triggers the injection of adrenalin into a salesman's bloodstream. Although it is impossible to define exactly the reason for a salesman being motivated by a competition, it is safe to say that most salesmen who want to win competitions want to do so for the honour and glory rather than for the prize. The value of the prize may be far less than the value of the commission they will have earned on their way to winning the prize.

I initiated competitions at two different levels, local and national. The local competitions were regular, on a weekly or monthly basis, the national competitions were usually based on performances over three months and were held only once or twice a year.

In most forms of competition, sport for example, the object is to recognize the achievement of the top athlete by presenting him or her with a gold medal and a cheque. Runners up receive a consolation prize of silver or bronze, the rest get nothing. Hundreds of sportsmen or athletes do not even bother to try to qualify for the contest because they know that there are probably sixteen outstanding performers who can justifiably feel they have a good chance of winning, and they are not in the same league.

No matter how large the gold medal, no matter how large the prize money, the overwhelming majority of athletes or sportsmen will not compete because they are realists. They know that no matter how much effort they put into competing, they could not finish up 'in the money' so it just is not worth the effort.

It is therefore very important to understand that sales competitions are very different from sporting events.

A sales competition is not designed to reward the best performer.

So what is it designed to do? It is designed to motivate the maximum number of salesmen to improve their performance and thereby achieve the maximum increase in sales. If it was seen to be an opportunity for the top 10 per cent of the sales force to earn valuable prizes or bonuses, almost 90 per cent would not be motivated by the competition and would not extend themselves to generate more business. The top 10 per cent who, by definition, already work very hard very effectively, may not be able to increase their sales appreciably above the norm and therefore the competition may do nothing more than pay the top salesmen a bonus for doing what they would have done anyway.

A sales competition, large or small, must be designed with one object in mind. The generation of the maximum amount of additional business.

I think the classic example of this is the Top Team Trophy which Edmund Barker, at Gross Cash Registers, initiated and which I developed. We had a very large sales force of some 500 salesmen and managers and we needed to motivate as many of them as possible to increase their sales effort in the three months running up to Christmas. You may be thinking that there is not a natural three-month period 'running up to Christmas' because the quarter runs from October 1st to December 31st.

Not only is that true, it lays down one of the basic rules for running a competition. It must be timed so that it generates false peaks. There are usually natural peaks which the remuneration schedule generates. If salesmen are paid commission monthly, they will go flat out at the end of each month to close as much business as possible. If they receive a substantial quarterly bonus the peaks at the end of March, June, September, and December are higher than those in other months.

As the last few days of a competition will certainly generate a peak, the closing date should be somewhere between the 10th and 20th day of the month.

The next ground rule is that the sales force must be kept up to date with the latest standings in the competition. A weekly bulletin with masses of rabbit about every member of the sales force on the leader board is the minimum acceptable level of communication. In an ideal world, every member affected by a change in the standings would be given an updated bulletin on a *daily* basis.

So the start and finish dates are agreed and they are timed to generate false peaks. Someone is given the job of keeping the records which will enable us to send out a bulletin every Friday evening.

The third ground rule is to involve the family.

It does not matter whether the competition is a weekly event involving five salesmen, or a national competition which involves the whole sales force, it should be designed to involve every salesman's family. This does not only mean that the prizes should be attractive to the salesman, his wife and children, but that they should know about it.

The occasional bulletin addressed to the salesman's partner will ensure that they do know about it. If the competition is designed to achieve the maximum increase in business, it must involve every member of the sales force.

Before I tell you about the Top Team Trophy, let us start at the bottom.

At Gross Cash Registers, I was involved in very large national contests which I have referred to and which I will explain later in this chapter, but when I resigned from Gross and joined Ansafone, I found that I was managing a small, unmotivated sales force with 20 per cent of them, who achieved 80 per cent of the business, based in London.

There were ten salesmen and two managers, London North and London South, based at the head office at 19 Upper Brook Street, London W1.

My office was very large, so I 'invited' every member of the London sales force to join me in my office every Friday afternoon at 3.30 p. m. They felt that this was an offer they could not refuse, so every Friday afternoon at 3.30 p. m. we met and we reviewed the individual performances of each salesman over the past week.

I am sure that I do not have to tell you that it is not a pleasant experience to be invited into the sales director's office, and sit there while he writes up on a flip chart the sales achieved by each member of the London sales force, if you have not made any sales that week. Even if the sales director makes no reference to the fact that you have had a blank week, even if your colleagues make no reference to the fact that you have had a blank week, it is not something that you would welcome next week.

So the first, most fundamental effect of a sales competition, is to identify the non-producers and either stimulate them into growth or identify them as a liability.

Inevitably there were a few (20 per cent) salesmen who always wrote more business than the other 80 per cent, so I had to find a way of getting the 80 per cent involved. You will naturally appreciate that competitions that give the prizes to the same people every week (on merit) do nothing to motivate the 80 per cent who know they cannot win anyway (they do not have the energy).

I decided to make the weekly competitions a combination of

achievement and chance. It was quite normal for a good salesman to make more than one sale per week and lamentably possible for the marginal salesman to sell nothing.

Therefore, when they gathered together in my office on Friday afternoons, I gave each salesman one raffle ticket for each sale he had made that week.

I then enlisted the help of an unbiased observer, usually my assistant, Jean Croft, to draw the winning ticket out of the hat.

The best salesman, with three tickets, had a tremendous advantage over the man with one ticket and the non-producers had to sit on the sidelines watching proceedings, with no chance of winning anything.

The prize had to fit the occasion, a weekly event among a comparatively few salesmen. It presented me with quite a problem and I would shop around madly in my Friday lunch time to find something suitable. I put a limit of £10 on the prize and I came up with driving gloves, coin holders, and countless other trivia, but the important, motivating factor was not the prize, was not the commission the salesman had earned by achieving that standard of performance, it was the recognition and the respect that the salesman earned from his peers. Sometimes I needed to give the whole sales force a shot in the arm without going 'over the top' and launching major national competitions. Christmas was a typical example. I do not have to tell you that in most industries it becomes increasingly difficult to maintain the same number of sales interviews per day as Christmas approaches.

I think there are three reasons for this. First, it is a fact that some people are very busy in the run-up to Christmas, the retail trade is an obvious example. 'I am too busy to see you before Christmas' is an only too common response you can get to a telephone call asking for an appointment in mid December.

A second reason is that most people have four weeks holiday nowadays and many have five. In most companies, holiday entitlement cannot be carried forward from one year to another, and therefore many people use up their holiday entitlement by taking the last week, two weeks, or even three weeks of the year off.

There is not a lot you can do about this, other than use the excuse to give you a full diary of appointments for the first two weeks of January, but the third reason is one we can do something about.

As Christmas draws near, the salesman reduces the number of hours and the degree of effort he puts into the job. It is so easy to accept the 'too busy before Christmas' objection, even if it is only the obvious, convenient way of preventing the salesman from getting an interview. We all know that 90 per cent of the 'objections to the approach' that we hear are lies, based on emotion and not on fact. For eleven months of the year we treat them accordingly, but come the season of goodwill we go soft in the head and believe this palpable lie. Maybe some salesmen *want* to believe that it really is impossible to book a full day's work during those pre-Christmas weeks because he needs a bit of free time to do the Christmas shopping without the children, and write the Christmas cards and buy the tree and, anyway, why should he not have a few hours off just before Christmas?

Unless you have a pair of jack-boots in your wardrobe, you will find it difficult to reject this philosophy out of hand, and yet you cannot possibly afford to lose one month's business in deference to a religious festival.

So what do you do?

What I did was organize a simple family contest that ran right up to Christmas Eve, and in which every member of the family could take part.

The idea occurred to me when I came across one of our children's puzzle books. There was a page on which were dozens of numbered dots. All you had to do was join the dots in numerical sequence and you drew a picture.

I am not sure how or why my mind took the giant step for mankind which made me draw a turkey and two bottles of wine in numbered dots, and made it possible for every member of the sales force to win a Christmas turkey and two bottles of wine by writing enough business in December to join all the dots together.

Although I have run many different competitions since then, in fact I am running a 'presents on the tree' competition right now, I believe this is the best one I have ever run for involving all the family and all the sales force. I was not asking for superhuman effort, I was asking for normal sales results in December. Obviously, it was the children in most cases who joined the dots together, first a drumstick, then the whole leg, and so on. The parents appreciated the fact that they would not have to buy a turkey and could also get a couple of bottles of wine to wash it down. Furthermore, it was all attainable. They could not be beaten out of a place by Mr Smartarse. Even if they did not do as well as they had hoped, they could win either a turkey or a turkey and one bottle of wine, and every night the children would be asking 'How many numbers can we join up tonight?'

Short, sharp competitions can be extremely cost effective. One year, when the Top Team Trophy competition had ended and there was a three-week interval before the results could be announced and the prizes awarded at the annual dinner, I introduced a three-week competition for branch managers. There were eighteen of them. I promised a mink stole to the manager whose branch business increased by the greatest percentage over the three-week period compared with previous performance. They went mad! I do not know how they motivated their branches, but I have a shrewd suspicion their wives had a great deal to do with it. That mink stole, in those days, cost £100, and it kept eighteen branches working flat out for three weeks, which would have been a slump, a reaction to the thirteen-week competition that had gone before.

But let me tell you about the Top Team Trophy, the TTT as it was always known. If you have read *The Secrets of Successful Selling* you will know a bit about it already. As the name implies, it was essentially and primarily a competition between teams, between branches. If you have a sales force that is divided up into teams or branches, the most important and influential members of your sales force (next to yourself, of course) are the branch managers. They select, they teach, they train, they motivate, they drive, they fire. They determine how much business the branch generates. Add them all together and they determine how much business the company generates.

I have always been very keen to generate branch identity, loyalty to the branch, and a responsibility to the branch manager. I have tried to inculcate a sense of friendly rivalry between branches, the kind of rivalry that exists between league football clubs. The managers are friends; in football terms they buy and sell players to each other, they appear on television together as commentators, but on the field the teams are constantly battling for survival, for promotion or relegation. The members of each club must support their managers and do all they can to help him and themselves move up within their division and, when possible, qualify for promotion.

So, the TTT set out to pit one team against another and by so doing involve every member of the sales force, new recruit or old lag, all loyal to their branch, their manager, motivated by a desire to share the glory of winning the TTT or avoid the shame of being the member of the team who let the side down and thereby denied them the chance of winning the coveted trophy.

You might well think that this simple concept would indeed motivate every member of the sales force and that there was no need to complicate it by the injection of other concepts. You would be wrong, because there were two dramatically different sectors of the sales force who were not motivated by this format.

The first was the high producing, hardworking, totally praiseworthy member of the sales force who was attached to a branch of donkeys . No matter how hard he worked, he could not carry the branch on his shoulders alone, so he switched off. A team contest was something he could not compete in.

The second was the donkey. If he was in a branch full of donkeys, he was well camouflaged, he could not be seen. He knew that neither he nor his branch would be mentioned in despatches and, even if they were, he would be invisible. If, on the other hand, he was in a dynamic branch he could bathe in reflected glory. He could ride to the winning post like a flea on a greyhound's back without having to exert himself.

I therefore introduced two additional 'motivators' directed towards these two totally disparate individuals.

The first was an individual contest so that the best salesmen were recognized as being the best. If they thought they were the best, they had to prove it.

The second was to stage the announcement of the winners at a top hotel with transport and accommodation arranged and paid for by the company for every *qualifying* member of the sales force, with his wife or partner.

Expressed simply, I arranged for a dinner, cabaret, and prize-giving at the Savoy, the Dorchester, the Park Lane Hilton, the Grosvenor House, the Grand, Brighton, etc. etc., at which the top teams received their awards and the top sales people received their awards, but every member of the sales force present at those presentations had earned their place by generating the basic quota level of business over the previous three months. Those that were not invited were due for dismissal.

The stage management of an event like this is all-important. I know that I am leaving myself open to all sorts of criticism, but I have to say that most salesmen and their wives have never stayed at a good London hotel. They have never had dinner at the Savoy or the Hilton, and never would have, had they not been invited by the company in recognition of the salesman's or saleswoman's above average performance. They would never be taken by luxury coach to see Windsor Castle or have the opportunity to spend a few hours in Harrods were it not for the Top Team Trophy.

My assistant, Jean Croft, and I worked hard but derived a great deal of pleasure from these logistically complex operations.

There was initially the definition of the vehicle that would carry the competition from launch to completion and I do not mean a luxury coach. I mean that the hard facts are that the winners in each class will be judged on the value of business they write, but to score a competition in those terms is unacceptable. There has to be a better, more interesting way.

I have already explained how I glamorized a £30 Christmas bonus by converting that £30 into a series of numbered dots which, when joined together, became the outline drawing of a turkey and two bottles of wine. Do you think there would have been the same fun, the same family involvement, if I had said 'Each salesman exceeding quota will be given £30'? Obviously not.

So it is with major competitions.

It does not matter whether the value of sales is expressed as:

- Climbing the Matterhorn.
- Golf at St. Andrews.
- World Cup football.
- Snooker at the Crucible.
- Tennis at Wimbledon.
- The America's Cup.

There has to be a vehicle which gives the organizer scope to write interesting weekly bulletins. You will remember that I have already referred to the importance of mentioning as many salesmen as possible by name. If you can say that Phil Anderer has potted the black for seven points, or Frank Furter has sunk his putt for an eagle at the fifteenth, it has much more motivational impact than Phil Anderer has written £27,203, and Frank Furter has written £20,201.

Obviously, the competitors need to know how the points, strokes, shots, feet, goals can be converted into sales value. I know this sounds crazy, but comparative sales values will not turn competitors on. Goals and strokes will. So we have to convert sales values into an emotive medium that will motivate salesmen to perform to their maximum ability, but then, to evaluate the efficacy of the experiment, we have to convert back to sales values.

Why bother, you may ask, to go to all this trouble. My answer is simple, 'To put some fun into life' and to provide a vehicle which can motivate everybody.

I have said 'everybody' but obviously what I really mean is every member of the sales force, or do I? Yes, I do mean every member of the sales force because by mixing an amalgam of branch loyalty, individual pride, and the fear of dismissal, every member of the sales force was motivated for a part of the three months over which the TTT ran each year.

Obviously the prizes, the kudos, the dinner, all had to be successful year after year. To get a feel of what it was all about you need to read Chapter 14 of *The Secrets of Successful Selling.*

So we can look at competition prizes that range from a pair of driving gloves to a holiday in Kenya, and see how they can be used to motivate people, but we must go back to my definition of motivation to see why competitions are successful.

I said motivation was 'Harnessing the ambitions of others to achieve mutual gratification'. Competitions allow salesmen and their employers to achieve mutual gratification because they generate additional business for the employer and:

1. Enable the salesman to earn the respect of his family and his peers.
2. Help him to identify with his branch, as a member of a team with which he would want to identify.
3. Enable him to enjoy a monetary gain.

But motivation is by no means confined to competitions. Although I talk about 'harnessing the ambitions of others for mutual gratification' you must remember that the 'mutual gratification' bit is purely for the overwhelming majority of employers who have to make a profit before they can afford to employ anyone.

Every employee must understand that unless he generates more income for his employer than he draws as remuneration for his work, he is a liability and must therefore expect to be sacked. Sometimes there is nothing you can do about this type of situation, but occasionally the *employee* could generate more income for his employer, and thereby safeguard his employment, if he was motivated to do so.

Competitions motivate some salesmen with a broad brush. You give them all the same or similar goals to achieve and some, maybe most, have 'an ambition' to win and therefore they are motivated. Others think competitions are a bore and therefore they are not motivated. It could be that this type of salesman cannot face the possibility of being seen to be less capable than some of his colleagues so, rather than compete and lose, he chooses not to take part. He saves face that way and can still say 'I could have won if I had wanted to'.

What can we do about this type of salesman, or any other for that matter, when there are no competitions, and we want to motivate them?

First, we must find out what their ambitions are, for motivation is harnessing the desire to achieve an ambition. I found that sometimes this was easy because they were only too anxious to tell me what their ambitions were, but this was certainly not always the case. When I was sales director controlling a large sales force, I was at least twice, and usually three times, removed from the salesman in the field.

There was his branch manager, who was closest to him, his regional manager, who spent some time with him, and a sales manager who knew him fairly well, but not well enough to know what made him tick. Obviously I had to delegate the responsibility of personal motivation to the branch managers while, at the same time, providing them with guidelines and a framework in which they could operate effectively.

I knew that if a branch manager was to learn the true ambitions of his sales force, he had to become involved with them on a personal level. They had a professional responsibility to teach and manage each member of their team but this was principally with regard to the improvement of their selling skills and maintenance of discipline, ensuring that a good week's work was performed and documented correctly. There was no requirement in their job specification for them to go further than that.

To start the ball rolling, I introduced this subject at one of our monthly management meetings and I called it 'management involvement'.

I gave every manager a personal record card for each member of his team. It was essentially a diary, a generous line for every day of the year, giving him enough space to write down what had happened that day with that salesman, other than the normal activities of manager and salesman.

This record card performed a dual function. It enabled the manager to see how often, or how rarely, he showed any personal interest in the salesman and, second, if the manager was showing an interest in what the salesman's ambitions were.

If you are currently controlling a team of salesmen would you be able to tell me, if I asked you, what your salesmen's ambitions are?

If not, you need to read these notes on 'management involvement' and get yourself some personal record cards, because unless you know what each member of your team is working for, you will not be able to help them achieve their ambitions.

Recognizing the importance of motivation, an American marketing consultancy asked 400 of the largest sales orientated companies if they could interview their top salesman. They told each company they approached that they were asking the same question of 400 top companies and each company would be given the results of their 400 interviews. All the companies approached agreed to the consultancy interviewing their top salesman, for they were all more than anxious to discover whatever they could about the make-up of the most successful salesmen in the country.

The salesmen were interviewed and asked a formidable range of questions. What did or does your father do for a living? Did you have a happy or unhappy home life as a child? What kind of car do you drive? How tall are you? How did you vote at the last election? How do you relax when you are not selling? What kind of records do you buy? What TV channel do you watch most of the time? What academic qualifications do you have? How many jobs have you had in the past seven years? Are you married for the first time, second time, or more than twice? Enter the number in the box. Do you smoke? Answer yes or no. Do you have a private income and, if so, how much per annum?

The questions seemed endless and often irrelevant, but at the end of the day, it was possible to determine if these 400 super salesmen came from some common mould that could be used to generate a steady, ready supply of potentially successful salesmen.

Unfortunately, these 400 successful salesmen did not fit into a common mould. On the contrary, they turned out to be cubes, spheres, pyramids, and every other type of definable solid object, so the survey looked like being a waste of time. But there was one question that proved to be the catalyst for successful motivation. It was:

'Why do you work so hard?'

The survey had shown that the 400 top salesmen had little in common with each other, but when this question was asked, 'Why do you work so hard?' every one of the 400 could give a good reason. The interesting fact was that the reasons they gave were all dramatically different.

One was working hard so that he would be noticed by senior

management and given the chance to earn promotion into management.

Another was paying off the debts he had incurred when the business he was trying to build failed.

Another was paying for his children to go to college.

One was repaying the money he had borrowed to buy a boat.

Another was indebted to the bookies.

One was saving up for a divorce.

Not only were all these 400 top salesmen able to say precisely why they worked so hard, the reasons they gave were personal to themselves. They represented their own short- or medium-term ambitions.

All the salesmen were motivated to work hard, so I tried to spread this philosophy throughout my own sales force by making every member of the sales force focus his attention on his own personal short- and medium-term ambition and then provide or create an environment in which this ambition could grow into achievement.

In Chapter 14 of *The Secrets of Successful Selling* I described the quarterly target cards that I issued to every salesman every quarter. These were not another form that had to be completed and returned to head office, but a private, personal thing which could be used by the salesman to help him to achieve his own personal short-term ambition.

They consisted of an A5 card divided into three parts by two vertical bold lines, so the whole thing could be folded up to cheque-book size and be carried in an inside jacket pocket. Alternatively, it could be left unfolded and pinned on the wall. The three sections represented three months and the card was ruled to give thirty-one days in each month along the bottom of the card.

The left-hand margin was scaled vertically to represent the value of business written during the three months period and the right-hand margin was scaled vertically to represent the salesman's gross income which corresponded with the value of business written as scaled in the left-hand margin.

This was a commonsense approach because nearly every ambition could be converted into money.

To make the system work, the salesman drew a line on the quarterly target card from the bottom left-hand corner diagonally upward to the point on the right-hand scale which represented the gross amount of money the salesman would need to sustain his present standard of living over the next three months.

He then estimated the amount of *additional* money he would need to earn during this quarter to achieve or be on target for his first goal. He scaled that up the right-hand scale and then joined that point by a straight line to the bottom left-hand corner of the card.

So we now have two lines emanating from the bottom left-hand corner of the card. One represents the level of income, and therefore sales, the salesman has to generate to sustain his present standard of living, the other shows him what he will have to do to achieve his goal.

For the card to work successfully the goal must be identified and *must* be the salesman's personal goal, not something the manager makes him accept as a goal. It is useless for the manager to say, 'Now this quarter, Charlie, I want you to be the top salesman in the branch. Now, to do that you will have to double your sales, so let's put two lines on your quarterly target card. One is what you are doing now, the other is twice what you are doing now. All you have to do is plot your sales day by day, week by week, on the chart and you will see how you are going towards fulfilling my ambition that you will be the best salesman in the branch this quarter'.

We have to get back to 'management involvement'. Keep a record of every contact you make with each salesman and what transpired outside the normal manager/salesman relationship. You will find that one is interested in sailing, another in travel. A third will be expecting their first child, another trying to buy their first house.

There are as many personal ambitions as there are people and, therefore, there will be some people who just want to be left alone and not bothered with quarterly target cards. Even they can be motivated by the promise that they will not be bothered by or required to complete quarterly target cards as long as they produce above-average performances.

This philosophy of promising that conformity is not required unless performance is below expectation is something that I put into practice at Gross Cash Registers during my first year. I had scarcely put my feet under my desk, when the annual dinner came around. I had met comparatively few of the managers, but they had heard about me and they knew that I was there to improve sales results from the existing sales force and to generate growth. Needless to say, some managers were not happy.

My wife and I sat at the top table on the sales director's right hand and the dinner was going swimmingly. We had all had enough to drink and the evening was moving relentlessly towards Auld Lang Syne when the manager of Brighton branch, Peter Bygrave, swayed up to the top table, looked me squarely in both pairs of eyes and said 'If you come to Brighton branch, I will make sure that there is no one there for you to meet'.

I said 'I have no intention of coming to Brighton branch while business remains good, but should it decline I will be there to find out why!'

Needless to say, Brighton branch had its bad weeks as did every other branch, so I had a legitimate reason to go out selling with Peter Bygrave before long. Within the hour and without the alcohol we were friends and I had one of my most memorable sales experiences that day.

We met at Guildford and started calling on a secondary shopping parade. This was very soon after my arrival at Gross, long before I had introduced the adding machine approach.

The official method of working in those days was to carry into every shop what was known as a 'small unit'. It consisted of a cash register drawer with a paper roll on top. I can't remember exactly how much it cost, but I believe it was £24.

We called on every shop and before long we were, or to be more precise Peter Bygrave was, giving a demonstration of a 'small unit to a gentlemen's hairdresser. The actual owner of the establishment was not there, but his son was. He recognized the merit in having a lockable till and an accurate record of each transaction, but he was a young Turk so he had to issue a challenge. He reckoned a thief could pick it up and run away with it, so he said that he would pay £20 for the till if he could catch Peter while he ran 200 yards up the road carrying the till, but if he could not catch him in 200 yards he would pay the full price of £24.

Peter and I looked at each other and there was total agreement between us without words. We collected our things together, gave the hairdresser's son a look that said 'Crawl back under your slimy stone' and we left.

Peter and I were friends thereafter and he continued to be one of the best branch managers in the Gross sales force.

But to get back to the quarterly target card.

I know that some salesmen pinned it onto the kitchen wall, and the family became involved every day in plotting the salesman's business, and therefore his path towards his personal goal.

Sometimes the children would mark the card, sometimes his wife.

One salesman did not use the card in its original form, but it prompted him to break down his personal ambition of buying a house, to get away from his in-laws, where he and his wife had lived ever since their marriage, into quarterly, digestible chunks. To keep the goal foremost in his mind, he photographed one of the houses they wanted to buy and sellotaped the photograph on the dashboard of his car. It was always there, always with him, staring him in the face every time he felt like knocking off a few minutes early.

He knew exactly how much deposit he needed and he knew how much business he had to write to raise the deposit within the year. He did not use this as his goal. He divided it into twelve separate, achievable targets, one to be reached each month. They were:

Month 1	Kitchen (the most important room in the house).
Month 2	Bedroom 1 (the second most important room in the house).
Month 3	Bathroom.
Month 4	Lounge.
Month 5	Dining room.
Month 6	Bedroom 2.
Month 7	Bedroom 3.
Month 8	Garage.
Month 9	Carpets.

Month 10   Kitchen appliances.
Month 11   Bedroom furniture.
Month 12   Lounge and dining-room furniture.

Let it be said they had some money saved already, so the targets were realistic and they visited the building site regularly, not to say, as many young couples were saying 'Wouldn't it be marvellous if we could afford one of these homes?' but to say 'Well, we have the deposit on the kitchen, bedroom and bathroom, so it must all be downhill from now on'.

Although motivation is harnessing ambition, I found that very often my salesmen did not realize that they could achieve ambitions that were within their reach, because they had been conditioned by their previous experience and the experience of their parents that detached houses, overseas holidays, and a second car were for the privileged members of society, not for them. How wrong they were. All it needed was for me to show them how a modest share of the *additional* income they were now enjoying could open up endless opportunities that were not open to them before.

Naturally, there were many salesmen who had always been used to a high standard of living, and a successful selling career enabled them to maintain that high standard. That was their motivation.

15

Remuneration

How should you pay salesmen?

The answer must be 'In many different ways'.

I have had to answer this difficult question many times and I have had to come up with the right answers for, in my opinion, the manner in which a sales force is paid can influence its effectiveness dramatically.

It influences the recruitment process, it influences the performance, it influences profitability, it influences the market.

The effects of remuneration are far reaching indeed.

There are almost as many variations on the theme as there are melodies that can be played on the piano, for the range of salary, commission, and bonus scales is at least seven octaves.

In my view there are also limits on remuneration packages beyond which I would never go. Rather than define those limits, let me go one step beyond. Straight commission is one step beyond, as is a straight salary. Between these two off-limit extremes everything is possible and I shall exploit the variations on the theme shortly, but let me just explain why I think straight commission and a straight salary are unacceptable.

Let us look at straight commission first.

You may think it strange that I should outlaw this method of remuneration when that was the way I was paid when I first embarked on a sales career with George Newnes. The truth is, it is because that is the way I was paid that I recognize it as an unacceptable method of remuneration. If you pay people on straight commission, no salary, no expenses, no car, they are self-employed. You do not employ them. If you tell them they must make five calls a day, they can put two fingers up at you. If you tell them they must follow up enquiries within twenty-four hours, they can put two fingers up at you.

Now, you may say 'Oh yes, but there are many responsible, honest, hardworking salesmen like you. You worked loyally for George Newnes on straight commission'.

Not true.

I sold a lot of encyclopaedias for George Newnes, but I did not work loyally. I was not employed by 'them'. I was self-employed. Even whilst I was working for them I had entered into partnership with two colleagues to form a business selling fruit drink dispensers.

If Newnes had not offered me promotion, I may well have become another Charles Forte or Conrad Hilton.

If you pay salesmen straight commission, you have no control over them whatsoever. You cannot give them field supervision when you want to, you cannot ensure they will attend sales meetings, you cannot ensure they will handle enquiries responsibly, and you can be certain that once they have been paid for making a sale, they will not give a damn what happens to that customer and will never make a follow-up call to ensure that all is well.

There is, however, one notable exception to this rule and that is where a self-employed agent is appointed to provide permanent representation and after-sales service for an established company and who is closer to being an authorized distributor than he is to a straight commission salesman, although he is paid an agent's commission and is not purchasing the product and then selling at a higher price as does a distributor.

Let me clarify this point, by citing two obvious examples.

First, there is the double glazing or encyclopaedia salesman who is paid straight commission and works on the hit-and-run principle. His employer has no control over him, he comes and goes as he pleases, and it is usually quite soon after he has come that he goes to pastures greener. This is unsatisfactory.

Second, there are the insurance agents. It is common for these salesmen to earn commission when they write the business, but also to nave an interest in future premiums. They also write additional business from the same clients so an ongoing relationship develops. Agents of this type need to be thoroughly vetted in every way before appointment and thoroughly trained afterwards. They are then perfectly satisfactory.

So let us now look at the straight salary option.

As was pointed out to me by Tony Cass at George Newnes, if you are paid a straight salary it must reflect average performance. The good salesmen subsidize the poor salesmen. But it goes much deeper than that.

You have to go back to the recruitment process.

If a salesman applies for a sales appointment that offers him £18,000 p.a. in 1999 as a straight salary and is prepared to accept that appointment with no opportunity to earn commission or bonus, then, as far as I am concerned, he is what is known in sales circles as a 'nose picker'. If he were a true salesman he would want the opportunity to earn £30,000 and would not expect anyone to pay him this as salary.

So we come to the middle ground and we have to decide the percentage of the total earnings that should be salary, or commission, or bonus, or share of profits.

My personal view is that salesmen should never be remunerated on share of profits, for whereas it may be true that the selling price is often within the salesman's control, there are in most cases many additional cost factors that are outside the control of the salesman. Profitability is not therefore a reasonable basis on which bonus should be calculated.

So, we come back to the need to define the salary, commission, and bonus content of any remuneration package, excluding straight commission, straight salary, and profit related schemes.

There are three variables:

1. The applicant.
2. The product.
3. The labour market.

Let us look at the applicant.

If you are looking for a man to sell local advertising space to local retailers, your applicant will be different from the man who will apply for the job of selling nuclear reactors to the Far East and the Americans.

So, first of all, you have to draw up an applicant profile.

This profile will include not only the amount of money he needs to have coming in every month to sustain his present standard of living, but also the additional income he would need to generate to ensure that he regards your company as the company he would want to work with for the foreseeable future.

This does not mean that you have to employ private investigators to determine the weekly or monthly commitments of every applicant, far from it.

You define the type of person you feel is suitable for the position you wish to fill and then offer the *lowest* salary you think the applicant would accept provided that the earnings potential is there to enable the applicant to enjoy the Walter Mitty life-style he has always visualized he should be living.

So the next standard you have to define is the Walter Mitty life-style as perceived by the applicants for the position you have to offer. Obviously, these standards will vary dramatically from the 22-year-old, living at home with his parents, to the 40-year-old with two children at public school.

You may think that the salesman's remuneration must be geared to the price of the product and the gross profit margin within which the employer operates. Not true. It is no use saying, 'I buy at 100, so I will sell at 200,' unless you show that your overheads and sales costs will be less than 100 and preferably less than 60.

Therefore, before you set your selling price you have to define in meticulous detail the manner in which the product or service must be sold and establish the true cost of selling the product.

So you don't take the cost of the product and then fix the selling price on an assumption that the product can be sold profitably with a mark-up of 50 per cent or 100 per cent. You establish just what it really costs to sell the product before you set the retail price.

The cost of selling the product must take into account all the sales overheads, including recruitment and sales management, and the cost of replacing unsuccessful recruits. There may also be trade discounts, allowances for part exchange, and other special factors which apply to a particular industry.

When you have done that you know what the selling price should be, what margins there are for offering discounts or accepting trade-ins, and what is the total amount of money available for remunerating an average salesman.

I have mentioned salary, commission, and bonus, but there are other very important components in the total remuneration package. The first is the car. Or is there a car? Naturally, some companies are not able to finance company cars so, in my view, because I do not want to engage self-employed people, a car allowance has to be paid in lieu. The second important component is a pension scheme, the third is paid holiday, the fourth is reclaimable expenses, the fifth is paid overseas holidays which sometimes masquerade under the title 'annual sales conference!' A sixth is staff perks, a seventh luncheon vouchers, an eighth is private medical insurance, either paid for by the company or offered at reduced rate through a group scheme. A ninth is share options, a tenth is . . . Need I go on?

The skill in cobbling together the right 'package' is in making the package fit the applicant so that the applicant you want accepts the job, while at the same time ensuring that it makes him work hard to achieve his own personal comfort level.

I know that some people do not consciously work for money. They work for kudos or promotion or the good of mankind, but, if they cannot pay the rent or buy their children new shoes, they will soon be looking for a better paid job. So let us ignore these paragons of virtue and accept the fact that we are going to be recruiting normal sinners like you and me, who enjoy the decadence of a capitalist society, and who are motivated by the opportunity to earn a lot of money, but who are, at the same time, responsible, law-abiding bread-winners.

You decide who the applicants will be by the way you structure your recruitment advertisement. Although there will be a few renegades who apply, the vast majority will take your advertisement seriously and react accordingly. If your advertisement invites applications from applicants with BSc. Eng. AMICE with not less than five years experience in the field of pre-stressed concrete beams, your applicants will all fit this job description within a margin of ±20 per cent.

If you advertise for ambitious young people between the ages of 18 and 22, who know they have the ability to communicate, who know they have the ability to earn £18,000 per year, then these are the people that will respond.

In most employer/employee relationships, the employer's aim is to achieve a fair week's work output for a fair week's wage. In the sales environment we are looking for a formula that will reward generously above-average performance, because once the basic quota level has been exceeded, the overheads have been recovered, and the total margin between cost price and selling price is available for distribution.

So, looking at the *applicant*, how do we (a) get him to apply for the job, and (b) motivate him thereafter?

Well, obviously the recruitment advertisement must be the vehicle that conveys to the potential applicant the vision of the job. The remuneration package will be a critical factor in the effectiveness of the advertisement.

Strangely, but not surprisingly, the salary, commission, and bonus may not be as influential as the company car.

In Gross Cash Registers and with Ansafone we originally provided sales and service staff with sign-written vans. The value of the advertising on the side of the vans was considerable, but no one would take the job!

We had to switch to cars, so you can see how important the company car, standing in the drive next to the Jones's, can be.

I am willing to bet that if you offered any number of applicants a basic salary of £20,000 but no car, or £18,000 p.a. plus a BMW 728i, the majority would go for the lower salary and the BMW. Your job is to do the sums and work out the most desirable package within the selling cost constraints which you have already established.

Naturally, as management, your first responsibility must be to the shareholders and therefore the return on the capital employed.

It necessarily follows that if you are able to pay a new recruit 100 units per sale but, due to his circumstances, he is willing to accept 50, then you pay him 50. Let me give you two factual examples of market forces applying:

1. When, some 40 years ago, I applied for my first sales job with George Newnes I was told that the commission on each sale was £5 and as it was comparatively easy to make ten sales per week I could earn £50 per week working about six hours a day. I had previously been working fourteen hours a day as an owner-driver to earn £40 per week. To me, the offer was very attractive. I accepted it and I was soon earning the extra money I had been promised. The point I am making is that my manager could have paid me £7 per sale, as he did subsequently, but there was no need for him to do so.

2. There are, unfortunately, a great many able people around in 1999 who have been made redundant for reasons outside their own control. This does not mean that every unemployed person is a suitable candidate for employment, but some of them are. Many middle-aged managers find themselves unemployable, too old to compete with young management applicants and too old to start again and learn new tricks.

    They often have lower monthly commitments than the younger men because their children are off their hands and are, in theory, no longer a financial burden (give or take a wedding or two). Furthermore, if they have not yet paid off their twenty-five year mortgage and many of them have, it is probably very small by today's standards. They may also have a little money put by, possibly through thrift over the years, but more probably the remains of a redundancy payment. On the other hand, they have usually become accustomed to a comfortable standard of living, two cars, overseas holidays, a bottle of wine now and then, and good shoes. Not only are they facing a bleak present, they are facing a bleaker future, because redundancy, early retirement, or the sack, call it what you will, means there will be no 50 per cent or 60 per cent of normal salary pension as a sixty-fifth birthday present.

Many of these capable people between the ages of 45 and 55 are prepared to accept almost any form of remuneration package from any employer who is prepared to pay them generously for excellence. In these circumstances, there is no need to pay more than a nominal salary to establish the 'employee' status, but then you can afford to wrap up the package in plenty of commission and or bonuses and a good car that he will not be ashamed of in his drive.

So, here we have two quite different situations where it is not necessary to offer all the money that is available in the budget to recruit suitable applicants.

Whereas I am advocating paying suitable applicants the lowest salary necessary to ensure that the applicant you want to recruit will accept the job you have to offer, I am not suggesting it should not be higher than your competitors are offering. I am merely saying 'Don't pay a higher *salary* than you need to recruit the man you want'.

I advocate this approach for three reasons. First, it motivates the salesman to write a lot of business to reach his comfort level. Second, it leaves you with a lot more money in the budget for commissions and bonuses, and third, your failures, and there will be failures, will not have cost you as much whilst they were failing.

So the applicant has to be taken into account when you are deciding the salary level you should offer, the commission and bonuses you can afford to pay, and the type of vehicle you should provide.

Now, let us consider how *the product* will affect the manner in which we construct a remuneration package.

The obvious factors that have to be taken into account are:

1. The price of the product and the frequency of sales.
2. The gross margin.
3. The discounts/concessions/trade-ins.

The price of the product and frequency of sales

I cannot think of a simple reason why, but the higher the price the less frequently you make a sale. The value of sales per year may be much higher with a high-priced product, but you make fewer sales.

If you employ a salesman to sell advertising space, he will make more sales per week if he is selling space in the classified advertisements than he will if he is selling television advertising campaigns.

If he is selling photocopiers, he will make more sales per month if he is selling the middle to bottom of the range of machines than he will if he is selling the highly sophisticated automatic feed and collation machines.

I suppose it is because there are more people with a small amount of money to spend than there are people with a lot of money to spend.

The value of the sale and the frequency at which sales are made are naturally going to affect the structure of the remuneration package.

The most critical factor is that the *average* salesman must be assured of sufficient income each *month*.

If we assume that the *average* salesman must receive £1,500 per month gross to meet his financial commitments, then the package must enable him to qualify for this minimum income *every* month if he performs satisfactorily.

If the product is fairly low in value but several sales per week are normal, then the salary can be minimal and commission, paid monthly, can be geared accordingly. Obviously, higher-than-average performance will earn him disposable income every month and it may be appropriate, if the margins will allow, to pay a quarterly bonus for consistent performance over the quarter. Bonuses for any period longer than one quarter are not usually cost effective.

Paying this type of salesman the lowest acceptable salary means that you can afford to pay a relatively higher rate of commission than you could if his salary were higher and this means that his earnings potential is greatly increased. Above-average performance is then generously rewarded.

If the product has a high unit value, sales may well be erratic, sometimes one or two sales per month and sometimes in bunches, with long intervals in between, like London buses. In these circumstances, a salesman with similar commitments would have to be paid a basic salary of £1,500 per month and then, normally, commission would be at a lower percentage. As a result, the potential earnings may be lower for the same volume of business, but not necessarily so.

Trade-ins and discounts

The trouble with any form of price concession is that it is usually negotiable. Sometimes salesmen are not allowed to give discounts or accept trade-ins without reference to their managers or head office. Obviously, in certain circumstances this is essential, but on balance I am in favour of giving the salesman the authority to give discounts or negotiate the allowance on a trade-in *provided* he knows *exactly* what he is allowed to do and *how it will affect his commission*.

I am in favour of him having this authority for two reasons. First, it enables the salesman to close the sale there and then without him having to make a telephone call or arrange to call back with an answer, by which time the prospect may well have placed the order with a competitor who could give an answer on the spot.

The second reason is that discounts and trade-ins can be a most valuable closing tool for the salesman, enabling him to use a 'concession' close.

A 'concession' close, as the name implies, means you make a

concession, you give the prospect *something to which he is not entitled*. Let me give you an example.

At Gross Cash Registers, we sold cash registers to shopkeepers, and nearly every one of them had a cash register already. We had to trade them out. Obviously, like secondhand cars, secondhand cash registers are old, worn, out of date, and hard to sell except to someone starting up in business for the first time, looking for something cheap.

We were trading-in secondhand machines at such a rate that there was no way we could sell them all ourselves, so we sold them to 'the trade' at trade prices, something between £10 and £25 each. Needless to say, the shopkeeper who had paid £100 for his machine some four or five years ago thought it was still worth about £50 and our salesmen had to trade these machines out at a realistic price.

The first thing we had to do was let the sales force know the true trade-in value of every machine, the price we could get for them if we sold them to the trade, but then give them a degree of flexibility so that they could close the sale by agreeing the trade-in price.

Obviously, the new machine was better and more expensive than the old one, usually about £200-£250, and we paid the salesman a range of commissions based on the *true* value of the sale. For example, if a salesman made a sale at the correct price of £250 he would receive commission of £50, if he gave a 10 per cent discount and accepted £225 his commission was reduced by 50 per cent of the concession to £37.50. There was a bottom price below which he could not go and his commission on such a sale was nominal, not worth the effort.

He then was free to do any deal he liked within the constraints of the trade-in price list and his commission schedule. If he did a deal with the trade-in coming in at its true value he lost no commission, but if he gave more for the trade-in than it was really worth then his commission was reduced in accordance with the commission schedule.

Naturally the salesmen became very professional at trading out machines at figures that were closer to the true value than the owner's imagined value. The technique they used was simple.

They would go about their job of selling the new machine and would present the price and the alternative ways of paying for it, ignoring the old machine completely.

Sure enough, sooner rather than later, the shopkeeper would say 'Well, what about the old machine? Will you take it in part exchange?'

The salesman would say 'Well, I could, but don't you think it would be a good idea to keep it as a spare for busy periods, like Christmas?' Normally, the shopkeeper would say 'Oh no, I wouldn't want to keep it. How much will you give for it?'

The salesman would reply 'Well, quite honestly, I would rather you told me what you think it is worth, because if I told you it is only worth a tenner (the truth) you would probably be offended'.

The shopkeeper, who had probably been thinking it was worth about £50 would then normally say 'I certainly would. I wouldn't accept that for it'.

The salesman would then say 'Well, that is why I said I would rather *you* told me what *you* think it is worth and if I can give it to you I will'.

The shopkeeper now knew that his machine was not worth £50, so he would say

'Well, I would have thought it was worth at least £30'.

The salesman would reply 'Well, I was afraid you would say something like that, but let's not fall out over £20. I will give you £30 and hope that I will find someone who is starting up for the first time and would be prepared to give me £30 for it'.

The sale was closed and the salesman would have his commission adjusted accordingly.

Sometimes he would be able to re-sell the trade-in for £30 and then his commission was restored.

I am not for one moment suggesting that salesmen should be encouraged to give money away, but if negotiation is an essential part of the sales process they should know exactly what they can and cannot do.

So you see putting together the right remuneration package is a complex and extremely important process. You have to take into account the person you want to recruit, the product you have to sell, and the state of the labour market.

At the end of the day, there are only three important considerations:

1. You must make your salesmen feel that they are being treated fairly, even generously.
2. They must be stimulated to achieve a high level of performance.
3. Last, but by no means least, sales costs must remain well within budget to allow additional sales promotional exercises, such as sales competitions as and when required.

16

Conclusion

I have been a Member of the Chartered Institute of Marketing for over twenty years. It was originally the Institute of Marketing and Sales Management, and I personally regret the day they changed their name and, by inference, implied that sales management is not as important as marketing.

I have never debated this point with the powers that be at the Institute, but I guess that they would say 'Marketing embraces sales. You cannot today say "Marketing and Sales Management" because it would be like saying "the whole family *and* the children", the children are part of the family, sales is part of marketing'.

Of course they are right. Sales is part of marketing, but having been both a sales and marketing director in my time, I think it is worth looking a little more closely at the sales *and* marketing, chicken and egg situation.

Although I try not to be guilty of plagiarism most of the time, I sometimes think it is better to say what someone else has said if I cannot think of a better way to say it.

So let me plagiaristically tell you about the sales manager and the marketing manager of a shoe manufacturer, who both went to a Third World country which will remain nameless to avoid the risk of precipitating an international political crisis.

Their brief was to conduct a market survey and telex their findings back to head office.

The marketing manager telexed 'Not a viable market, 90 per cent of the population do not wear shoes'.

The sales manager telexed 'Fantastic potential, only 10 per cent of the population have bought shoes to date'.

Now, while I accept when I wear my marketing manager's hat that the road to commercial success is paved with the identification of a need, the development of a product or service that fills that need, and the means of bringing the two together, my view of the situation is different when I wear my sales manager's hat.

Naturally, I agree whole-heartedly with the marketing manager's view of the market. Within his terms of reference the sales manager's job is to take the product or service, which the marketing manager has defined, to the market, which he has identified, and persuade the potential buyer who has the potential need to buy his product. You cannot argue with that. But wearing my sales manager's hat, I see the sales function as being broader than that.

I see salesmen as missionaries.

Now, before you jump to the conclusion that I am an evangelist or that I hold 'inspirational' meetings every Monday morning, which I do not, let me give the *Chambers Dictionary* definition of a mission:

> An act of sending, esp. to perform some function: a flight with a specific purpose, as a bombing raid or a task assigned to an astronaut or astronauts: the errand or purpose for which one is sent: that for which one has been or seems to have been sent into the world: a sending out of persons on a political or diplomatic errand, for the spread of religion, or for kindred purpose.

Now, what did all these definitions have in common? I'll tell you. The person on the receiving end did not recognize he had a need for the product or service that the missionary was delivering.

Was the person on the receiving end of a bombing raid aware of a need?

Were the little green men on the moon aware of a need? Are the heathens, visited by missionaries, aware of a need?

The answer is 'no'.

So, whereas the marketing manager identifies the needs, the potential buyer is aware of, the sales manager identifies needs that the potential buyer is not aware of.

As I have said before, he finds a happy man who is content, makes him discontented so that he can make him content again.

This sounds very cynical but I do not mean it to be so. All my life I have been talking to people who were blissfully unaware of the opportunities they were missing through lack of information.

Probably the most dramatic example in my experience was during the 1960s when I was selling shelving as sales manager of Beanstalk. There were tens of thousands of retailers gradually starving to death as a result of the spread of supermarkets to every high street, blissfully unaware, or should I say desperately unaware, that they could survive if only they banded together in groups and converted to self-service.

I was a missionary in those days. The retailers whom I and my sales force called on did not want to buy shelving, they had shelving. They also had counters that kept the shoppers away from the shelves and the goods on them.

They needed a way to survive and that is what we sold them, a way to survive – and prosper. They thought they had no need for shelving, but they bought shelving because that was how they were able to fill their need to survive.

The road to successful sales management is a long one. It starts with the identification of a need and ends with the fulfilment of that need. It embraces all the matters I have discussed superficially in these few chapters and a great deal more besides.

If you have learned anything new from my experiences of sales management, I recommend that you beg, borrow, but preferably buy, other books on sales management so that you can choose from a variety of sources the techniques of sales management, that you feel will suit you best. I wish you well.

Index